Quilts and Quiltmakers
Covering Connecticut

The Connecticut Quilt Search Project

Schiffer Publishing Ltd®

4880 Lower Valley Road, Atglen, PA 19310 USA

Dedication

This book is dedicated to all Connecticut quiltmakers; past, present, and future.

Library of Congress Cataloging-in-Publication Data

Quilts and quiltmakers : covering Connecticut / the Connecticut Quilt Search Project.
p. cm.
ISBN 0-7643-1472-6 (pbk.)
1. Quilts--Connecticut. I. Connecticut Quilt Search Project.
NK9112.Q55 2001
746.46'09746--dc21
2001003937

Cover Quilt: Eagle Medallion, c. 1840-1865, made by the Keeler Family, Ridgefield, cotton, 77.5" x 78". Owned by Danbury Scott Fanton Museum and Historical Society, Inc. In 1697, Ralph Keeler was one of the first colonists to purchase land to settle a plantation. Ridgefield was the seventh town settled in Fairfield County.

Designed by Bonnie M. Hensley
Cover design by Bruce M. Waters
Type set in Bernhard Modern BT/Aldine 721 BT

ISBN: 0-7643-1472-6
Printed in China

Published by Schiffer Publishing Ltd.
4880 Lower Valley Road; Atglen, PA 19310
Phone: (610) 593-1777; Fax: (610) 593-2002; E-mail: Schifferbk@aol.com
Please visit our web site catalog at **www.schifferbooks.com**
We are always looking for people to write books on new and related subjects. If you have an idea for a book, please contact us at the above address.

This book may be purchased from the publisher. Include $3.95 for shipping.
Please try your bookstore first. You may write for a free catalog.

In Europe, Schiffer books are distributed by
Bushwood Books
6 Marksbury Avenue; Kew Gardens; Surrey TW9 4JF England
Phone: 44 (0) 20 8392 8585; Fax: 44 (0) 20 8392 9876; E-mail: Bushwd@aol.com
Free postage in the UK. Europe: air mail at cost.

Contents

©Amy Duggan

The State of Connecticut

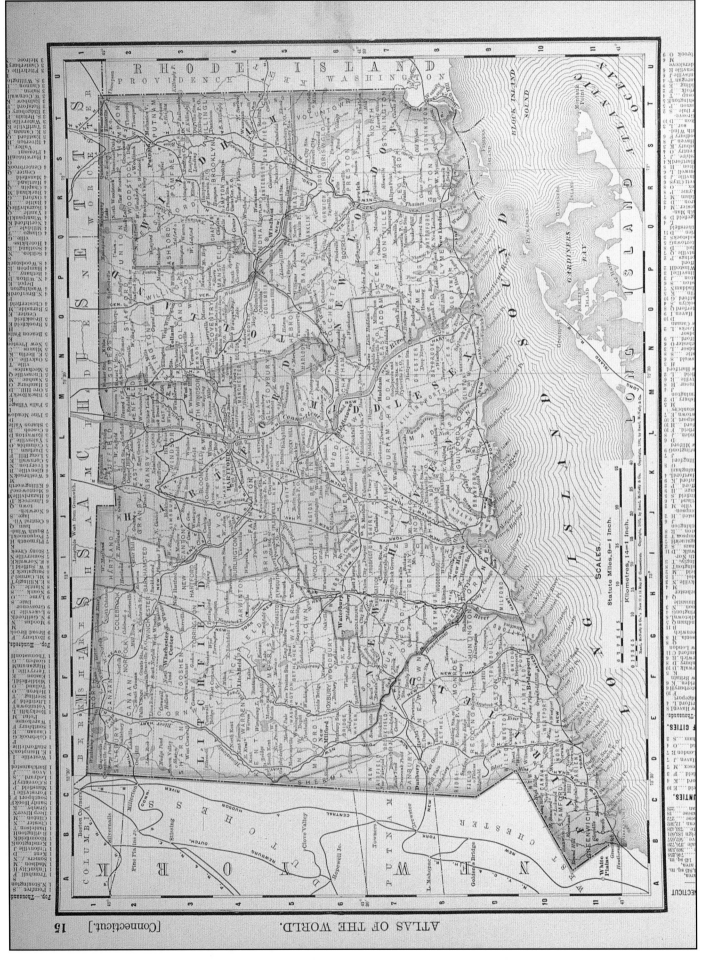

1895 Rand McNally map of Connecticut.

Acknowledgments

From its inception, the Connecticut Quilt Search Project (CQSP) has been a grassroots effort open to anyone with an interest in quilts. Beginning with the initial core of organizers, the project spread to include numerous volunteers and supporters sharing their time, money, expertise, and hospitality. The accomplishments of this Project are due to those volunteers and supporters. In addition, the Project could not have existed without the quilt owners, museums, and historical societies who generously shared their quilts and their stories.

Special recognition goes to the original organizers headed by Judy White and to the past officers, directors, committee chairpersons, and volunteers without whose vision and hard work this Project would not have been possible. For those who have moved on to other endeavors, we want to express our sincerest appreciation and please know that your contribution will not be forgotten.

Classes were held to educate Project members. Teachers included: Barbara Brackman, Diane Fagan Affleck, Dr. Margaret Ordonez, Sally Palmer Field, Eugenia Barnes, and Dr. John Sutherland. They prepared us to respond to the challenge of documenting quilts and taking oral histories.

CQSP held events and fundraisers to raise money to cover the cost of materials, film, and film development. A raffle quilt made by The Meetinghouse Quilters of Washington and one made by the Enfield Quilters of Enfield added needed funds. Other fundraisers included a cookbook, logo pins and earrings, orphan block sales, and slide shows. A special thanks goes to shop owners and the quilt show producers who graciously allowed us to sell items and promote quilt history awareness.

Our partnership with *Yankee Magazine* in their Community Partners Program deserves special recognition. The program began with a feature about CQSP in the November 1998 issue of *Yankee Magazine*. Nancy Trafford, Senior Community Partners Program Manager and Christine Salem, Consumer Marketing Director, coached and guided our efforts. Their support along with the incentives offered with a *Yankee* subscription resulted in an extremely successful fundraising campaign.

We truly appreciate the efforts of Marla Truini and The Country Players of Brookfield for their benefit performance of *The Quilters*.

A Gala was held at Shepaug Valley High School to showcase many of the documented quilts. Lenka O'Conner performed vignettes from her role in the Broadway play *The Quilters*. Fairfield Processing of Fairfield, Connecticut, showcased their nationally known fashion show. Vendors of fabric, books, stencils, and antique quilts provided interest for the attendees, and there was an auction of donated items.

The New England Quilt Museum and the Vermont Quilt Festival also held exhibits of Connecticut quilts. Without the Quilt Museum and people like Richard Cleveland, Chairman of The Vermont Quilt Festival, CQSP would not have been able to spread the knowledge of Connecticut quilts. In June 1996, Susan Fiondella represented CQSP at Sturbridge Village's symposium entitled, "What's New England About New England Quilts." Terri Nyman, Editor of *Ladies Circle Patchwork Quilts*, thought so much of the Project that she featured CQSP in an article "Partners for Preservation," written by Barbara Wysocki, in the February 1997 issue of *Ladies Circle Patchwork Quilts*. There was also a presentation made by Sue Reich at Quinnipiac's Annual Women's Creativity Conference in 1996.

Many thanks to the following for their support and sponsorship for this book: The Andre and Elaine Suan Foundation, Denise Fucini, Mrs. Thelma Woodbridge, Patches and Patchwork, and Fairfield Processing.

For assistance with research, we extend our appreciation to the many Connecticut libraries, historical societies, museums and newspapers. Special appreciation goes to Virginia Gunn for reading our manuscript and to our own in-house editor, Maureen Gregoire, whose level-headedness, attention to details, and organizational skills brought this book to reality.

We express our appreciation to all the Connecticut quilt guilds for their enthusiasm in sponsoring Documentation Days, providing many volunteer hours, and generous financial support during the past ten years. Special thanks goes to Mystic Color Lab, Mae Schmidle, Richard D. Wolff, Clay Winter, Carla Bue, Jean Potetz, Carla Kazanjian, Peter Costas, and the Portland Library.

Most importantly, sincere thanks to Peter and Nancy Schiffer of Schiffer Publishing and to Bruce Waters who expertly photographed our quilts as we did our best to educate him about Connecticut trivia. To our hard-working, most helpful, and very patient editor, Donna Baker, we express our gratitude.

The Connecticut Quilt Search Project Book Committee
Marilyn Cocking, Wanda Stolarun Dabrowski, Susan Fiondella, Maureen Gregoire, Cynthia Warren Mahdalik, Sue Reich, and Elizabeth Tishion

Snowball. A fundraising quilt made by The Enfield Quilters to benefit CQSP.

The Charter Oak. A fundraising quilt made by The Meetinghouse Quilters to benefit CQSP.

Introduction

by Barbara Wysocki

*I*f the aim of this book was literally to cover Connecticut, it would contain instructions for a quilt one hundred miles wide and sixty-two miles long. The batting would have to rise 2,380 feet to reach the slopes of Mount Frissell and be light enough to float on the Connecticut River, which bisects the state from north to south. More than three million people would be sheltered beneath such a quilt. To reflect the state's history and diversity, the quilt would need a rainbow of colors and an endless palette of patterns. An absurd and impossible task—no one would undertake a project of that magnitude.

Yet in many ways this book has an even greater challenge. It sets out to share the beautiful quilts found and the wealth of data gathered by the Connecticut Quilt Search Project. The group's statewide quilt documentation effort was a task of large proportions, including:

20 public Documentation Days,
26 historical societies, museums, and private collections,
800+ volunteers to assist in documenting the quilts,
3,058 bed coverings documented, including quilts, tops, comforters, and summer spreads.

The Connecticut Quilt Search Project compiled charts and graphs that illustrate where and when the quilts were made. Their work included how the quilts were set and if they were signed and/or dated. Over sixteen different construction techniques were noted and fiber content for the top, batting, and backing was documented whenever possible. Quilting stitches and patterns were observed and contrasted. By the end of the first phase of the project, sixty-eight binders had been filled with documentation records and slides. Later the Project contacted local collectors and museums around the country to add to their knowledge of quilts having a Connecticut connection. There is plenty of evidence attesting to the exhaustive nature of their inquiry.

These statistics are very valuable. Not only because they add to an understanding of textiles in general, but also because CQSP set out "To document and preserve histories of Connecticut quilts and quiltmakers." These personal stories could then be placed in the context of Connecticut and United States history. The data is a framework, almost an outline, of the development of a state and a nation, with an accent on women who made all but four of the quilts they viewed. The book fills in the details of this outline. It fills them in with careful research fueled by an ardent curiosity about the people who made quilts that were both fine and functional. These quilts have survived many decades, in many cases more than a century, and they lead the way to quiltmakers who mirror the social, cultural, and economic diversity of Connecticut's past.

The enduring care that went into every quilt does not require explanation, but the stories that accompany each quilt add more than facts to the visual experience. Because quilts are very personal and the work of someone's hands, and are usually made to warm someone, they may seem of less consequence than more durable works of art. Yet the very fact that these quilts survive and prompt such exhaustive examination proves their worth as conduits to the past.

It is fortunate that the Connecticut Quilt Search Project did not stop with the numbers. Beyond the colors and shapes that form such a memorable catalog of quilts, they looked for the quiltmakers whose lives were equally varied and richly textured. There's no way to know whether the quiltmakers whose quilts fill these pages ever thought about the quilt lovers of the future. Yet their quilts have touched modern hearts and opened twenty-first century minds far beyond measure.

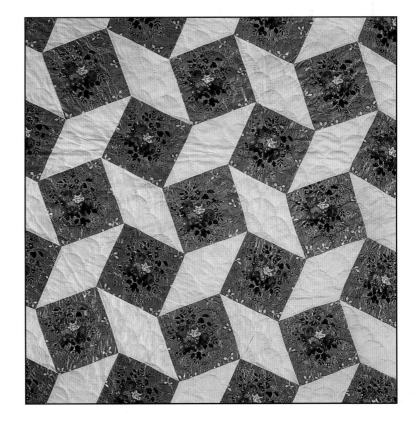

Historic Sampler

by Sue Reich

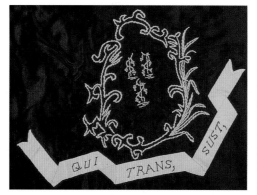

Researching quilts usually requires reexamining the lives of the women who made them. Covering three hundred years of history that these quiltmakers' lives span is a monumental task. Information about the lives of most women is like the fibers in a strand of thread, which can only be identified with microscopic vision. Women's stories don't leap out of the pages of history books. Often, they can only be gleaned by exploring accounts of their fathers or their husbands. Early families were large, demanding that most womanly energy be focused on the needs of day-to-day living. Seemingly lackluster at the time, that unrecorded daily activity is the information most sought after by quilt researchers today. As their stories unfold, the patterns of these women's lives give texture to the story of Connecticut.

Living in community was the single most important factor that dominated the lives of Connecticut women. In the early years, the words colony, congregation, meetinghouse, common, village, muster, gathering, and bee were used continually in their everyday dealings with one another. These were independent and self-reliant folk but they also had a great need for each other within the larger group. Joined together, they made quick work out of the larger tasks. The jobs of barn raisings, corn husking, wool picking, apple paring, spinning, and quilting were frequently organized as *bees*. Together, they also shared discourse, good fellowship, food, drink, and often dance.

During Connecticut's first three centuries, people were consumed with the production of cloth for clothing and providing warmth for their large families. The strong arms of the men were enlisted to shear the sheep and "break and swingle the stubborn flax fibre, cleanse and separate the matted fleece."[1] The gentler touch of the women raked and carded the natural fibers. The oldest, youngest, and the least able were put to work winding the quills and turning the reel. The matron of the house and her grown daughters worked at the spinning and wove at the looms. The products of their labors were the various weights of cloth needed by the family. "Sheeting, toweling, blankets, coverlets, heavy woolen cloth for winter and tow-cloth for summer, linsey-woolsey and gingham were all made at home."[2]

Daily practices die slowly in New England and the use of homespun was no exception.[3] In many cases, the everyday needs were still being met by homespun production. Despite the development of factories throughout the state, the wearing of homespun garments continued through

Oak Leaf and Reel, c. 1840-1865, made by Susan Alice Barnum (1833-1896), cotton, 98.5" x 80". Owned by Danbury Scott Fanton Museum and Historical Society, Inc. Born on October 4, 1833, Susan Alice Barnum lived her entire life in the Danbury and the New Fairfield area. Susan never married or had children. Her gift to posterity was this beautiful red, green, and white quilt with a vining red bud and maple leaf border.

the 1840s and saw resurgence during the Civil War years.

"Women, fear not, for thou shalt see the day,
When I, yes, I the vapor that I seem,
Of fire and water born, and baptized Steam,
Will save you all this labor: I will gin
Your cotton first, -then will I card and spin,
Reel, wash, dry, spool the filling, size the warp;
Nay if with both your eyes look out sharp,
You'll see me fling it so that both your eyes
Shall fail to see the shuttle, as it flies.
And, as the shuttle shoots, the reed shall strike:
I'll drive them both, and drive them both alike,
And, when the web is through the loom, by dint
Of my own power, I'll calendar and print!
Ay, madam, through these labors will I go,
And give your daughters printed calico."[4]

Progress also brought disadvantages and an unalterable return to past ways. While the ever-increasing mills rendered wealth and prosperity for some, the need for workers sent the youngest members of society into the dark, expansive buildings, unheated in the winter and poorly ventilated in the summer, laboring six days a week tending to their bobbins. In Glastonbury, the Roaring Brook provided power for one of the first large textile manufacturing establishments in Connecticut. In 1836, there were 5,200 spindles and 135 looms in production. One hundred and thirty girls and forty men comprised their employee roll call.[5] By 1845, seventy males and 120 females were running 5,690 spindles.[6]

Besides the thriving textile mills, there were many other textile-related industries in the state by 1870. Some of these included thread, needle, sewing machine, thimbles, sewing tables, and sewing attachments. Forty thousand residents of Connecticut attending the 1876 Centennial Exhibition in Philadelphia must have been proud of the state's representation of its textile industry. At their peak of greatness, the Willimantic Linen Company, makers of cotton thread and cotton ready-mades; Cheney Silks; Meriden Woolen; Hockanum Company of Rockville, maker of cotton warp cassimeres, flannels, and diagonals; the Howe Company, maker of the first sewing machine; Wheeler & Wilson Mfg. Company, maker of the lock-stitch, sewing machine; and the Weed Sewing-Machine of Hartford were just a few of the many textile-related exhibitors from Connecticut.

The mid-nineteenth century was an era of economic growth, abundance, and prosperity for Connecticut. No longer tied to an agrarian lifestyle, women had more leisure time to meet in groups and do needlework. Relieved of their former domestic drudgeries, influenced by literature that was both educational and creative, living in a time of continued inequalities toward females and blacks, and with husbands that still overindulged in spirits, what do you think the conversations around the quilt frames were? Writing in 1914, Mary Caroline Crawford recollects her memories of the quilting-party:

No gathering in the whole year
compared with the quilting-party as a
gossip-fest…the participants were all
close together inwards as at a square
table, many things which could be
whispered here first found
breath…Whether the cause be the
gossip or the collation, I find my
woman-soul yearning, as I write
these words, for a revival of the
quilting-party.[7]

Societal etiquette strongly encouraged membership in civic organizations. Unless the organization was all female, however, women could not become involved in the open discussion and had to pass their questions to the Chair, which was a man. One socially acceptable female public display of support was signing one's name to a petition. For centuries, women had expressed their love and care for their families through the production of cloth and quilts. It was only natural that now large numbers of women not only made quilts protesting the ills of society, they also placed their names on quilts made to support and raise funds for various causes and concerns. These time-honored bed coverings became fabric petitions, which gave a voice to women who were not yet allowed to register their vote. Through their quilts, women actively participated in changing the important social issues of their time.

The Colonial Revival that sparked a renewed interest in quilting during the 1920s, 1930s, and 1940s was a retreat to a time of contentment and peace. The economic uncertainty of the Depression years and the threat of another catastrophic war found people looking back at the past ancestral ways—the comfort zone of what was old and familiar. Celebrations marking the 200th and 300th anniversaries of Connecticut towns included pageants, parades, and exhibits featuring "the relics of antiquity." A resurgence in quiltmaking with displays and contests of colonial quilts occurred. Widely circulated women's magazines contained patterns that were adaptations of colonial designs. The nineteenth-century Mosaic, for example,

Cotton Factory village, Glastenbury.

Woodcut from *History and Antiquities* by John Warner Barber, 1836.

9

Stereo Optic Viewer card of the Cheney Brothers Mills showing women reeling the silk warp through a machine called a "Ferris Wheel."

Trade card from 1881 extolling the virtues of "The Best Thread for Sewing Machines."

Trade card from 1889 for the Wheeler & Wilson sewing machine made in Connecticut. Touted as the "only perfect sewing mechanism for family use."

Quilt show and silver tea given by the women of the Derby Methodist Church, January 30, 1938. *Photo by Vera K. Kneen.*

Trade card for Willimantic Thread, used not only to sell thread, but also to promote women's issues of the times, such as temperance and suffrage.

became the twentieth-century Grandmother's Flower Garden. The ever-popular Sunburst or Sunflower might have been the precursor of the Dresden Plate. The Orange Peel design found in Connecticut's earliest quilts became more challenging when made into a Double Wedding Ring. The Project's data, however, found that Connecticut quiltmakers of the beginning of the twentieth century produced fewer quilts than their counterparts in other states.

World War II further slowed quiltmaking in the state. The women of Connecticut were once again called upon to staff the defense industries in support of yet another war. Mail order catalogs, easily available ready-mades, and sewing machines purchased on payment plans provided for life's necessities and comforts in a much simpler and less time consuming way. Many women, however, made quilts as a diversion while their men were away and as fundraisers to support the war effort, as they did in WWI. After the war, the quilting boom subsided, although some women continued to quilt, particularly in rural areas and in homes where quiltmaking was a tradition. The twentieth century Connecticut goodwives who quilted kept true to the thriftiness of their ancestors by not wasting, by using up scraps and making do. They also quilted for special occasions or to commemorate a special event. A quilt made for Polly Hall's 1946 wedding demonstrates one of the best uses of scrap bag fabrics. Frugal Sarah Eva Watrous Pomeroy used as her quilt backing woven cotton that once covered the wings and fuselage of 1930s airplanes. Both are a sampling of the types of quilts made during the time when fewer Connecticut quilts were made.

Back in 1893, a group of Connecticut women known as the Lady Managers was asked to prepare an exhibit at the World's Fair representing the women of their state. This event, held in Chicago, was also called the Colombian Exposition. Given certain parameters to guide their choices, the Lady Managers identified and subsequently portrayed three essential virtues symbolizing the Connecticut woman: The first was to illustrate the fine spirit that lies beneath her face and fabric. The second was to demonstrate the industry with which she lived her life, and the third was to make evident her beneficent works in social and educational affairs.[8] Over one hundred years later, this book has attempted to uncover the lives of Connecticut quiltmakers. As their stories unfold, these same three noble qualities appear time and again. Indeed, you will find that what makes a Connecticut quilt is not the final result, but the essence of the quiltmaker whose hand silently guided the needle that stitched the quilts covering Connecticut.

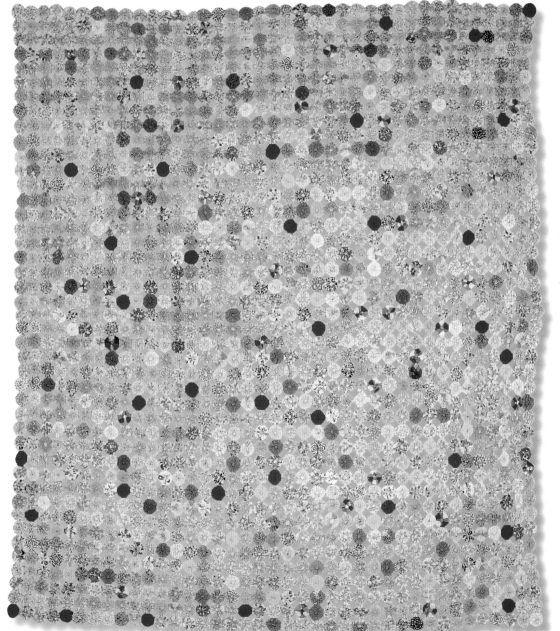

YoYo, c. 1945, made by Mary Moran Burns (1911-1992), West Haven, Connecticut, cotton, 79" x 87". Owned by David and Lorraine Burns.

Connecticut Quilts and Quiltmakers

by Wanda Stolarun Dabrowski, Susan Fiondella, Marie MacDermid,
Cynthia Warren Mahdalik, Peg Pudlinski, Sue Reich, and Elizabeth Tishion

Mary Geer Denison

The importance of record keeping and of signing quilts can only be reinforced with the story of Stonington's Mary Geer Denison. She and her husband, Elijah, had no children to carry on their heritage. Fortunately, due to the excellent genealogical histories of the Geer and Denison families, plus a signed and dated quilt kept at the Faith Trumbull House in Norwich, the name of Mary Geer Denison will not be lost.

This pre-Revolutionary War quilt of wool embroidery on linen gives a glimpse of the many quilts that must have been given up for the War effort. Mary cherished her fabric work of art enough to sign and date it *"MG Mary Geer, 1759."* The linen is most likely homespun. It was recorded in Stonington that "the wives and daughters of the planters spun and wove all of their linen and woolen cloth."[1] Before the mills were constructed in 1760, weave shops were established in the area. Operated out of homes and farms, they could alleviate some steps of cloth production.[2]

Mary was born to Ebenezer and Prudence Payson Wheeler Geer of Stonington on the family homestead in North Groton on September 24, 1739.[3] Her parents were successful farmers. The inscription on the gravestone of her father in the old Episcopal cemetery in Ledyard immortalizes his character that must have set the standards for the rest of his family. It reads: *"In memory of Ebenezer Geer, who lived virtuously and died hopefully."*[4] Mary was the third child of ten children born over a span of twenty years. As the first daughter with seven younger siblings, Mary's household responsibilities may have delayed her own marriage. In 1751, eight years before she made her quilt, four of her brothers died in one month from a scarlet fever epidemic. Mary's Center Medallion Embroidered quilt is dated 1759, when

Mary was age twenty. Mary remained single for another twelve years until, at the age of thirty-two, she wed Elijah Denison of Preston in 1771. Geer genealogical records state they left "no issue" (were childless).[5]

The linen, medallion center panel of Mary Geer Denison's quilt is embellished with carnations, thistle, clover, and other wild flowers of Connecticut. A remnant of the same linen used in the quilt's center extends to the first border, thus suggesting

both of these pieces had a previous purpose. The remainder of the first border is worked with crewel embroidery very different from the center panel. Dark brown floral chintz, with its sheen still intact, provides a frame in the second border. Finished with a coarse, brown monochrome print, the quilt's last border is in multiple widths. The backing of the quilt is unbleached linen. The quilting is executed in a parallel chevron design.

Center portion of quilt embroidered with Mary Geer Denison's initials and date.

Medallion with Crewel Work, 1759, made by Mary Geer Denison (1739-1827),
Stonington, cotton and linen, 94" x 98". Owned by Faith Trumball Chapter,
Daughters of the American Revolution.

Beulah Galpin Merriam

Many quilts can catch the eye with bold colors or powerful graphics, but few can catch the heart with a stronger voice than the *"Bethia Quilt."* Brought to the Project's last public Documentation Day, it quickly became one of the stars of the day. Its subdued colors, consistent with the era in which it was made, gave no hint of the heritage behind it. Nor did its graphics create any excitement. It was the story of a love that transcended time, and of nearly two hundred years of descendants honoring an ancestor's wishes that brought this quilt to the forefront. Here, taken from family records that date back to the turn of the nineteenth century, is its plaintive song.

The Revolutionary War was drawing to a close as Ephraim Merriam, a fifer in the Continental Army, longed for a reunion with his fiancée, Bethia Berry of Wallingford. However, the reunion he was soon to experience eclipsed anything he had in mind.

One night, while asleep in his tent, he was suddenly awakened by the spectral image of Bethia, dressed in her wedding gown. Certain that he was mistaken, he woke his tentmate, who verified the ghostly appearance. A shaken Ephraim feared that some great harm must have befallen his intended, so he made note of the hour and the day. In the next mail from home his worst fears were confirmed. Bethia had died at the moment he had seen her vision. Heartsick, Ephraim completed his service to his country and returned to his hometown of Wallingford.

As we know, time heals all wounds, and Ephraim eventually married Beulah Galpin on February 12, 1784, but he had not forgotten his first love. He gave the fabric that had been intended for Bethia's wedding dress to Beulah, and implored her to make a quilt. Beulah obeyed her husband's wishes, and used Bethia's fabric for the center panel and fabric from a dress of her own (possibly her wedding dress) to make this memorial quilt.

Pre-Revolutionary War dress fabric used for center portion of quilt.

Medallion, c. pre-1800, made by Beulah Galpin Merriam, Wallingford, cotton, 94" x 97". Owned by Bethia Currie.

Ruth Benton Thompson

Ruth Benton was born on February 2, 1742, the eighth child of Ebenezer and Esther Cruttendon Benton's nine children. On June 1, 1767, Ruth married James Thompson of Goshen, a town where, in the eighteenth century, the sheep outnumbered the human residents.[1] James was the fifth child of Deacon Gideon Thompson, prominent in the Goshen Congregational Church. Ruth and James raised seven children and family records recall the entire family's active participation in their farm's wool industry. The Thompsons typified the discourse of Connecticut's famous nineteenth-century orator, preacher, and philanthropist, Horace Bushnell, about the days of homespun. One's farm and property were not looked upon as a reflection of *fortune* but as an indication of *worth*: "The house was a factory on the farm, the farm a grower and producer for the house."[2]

In addition to family members, the Thompson household also had the help of two slaves, a fairly common custom in wealthy households of pre-Revolutionary War Connecticut. Old Chloe and her husband, Old Hess, were treated well by the Thompson family. Eventually, they were freed and given a house, a barn, and lands to cultivate.

In 1890, Ruth's grandson, the Reverend Dr. A.C. Thompson, told the following story at the 150th Anniversary of the First Congregational Church of Goshen: During the harsh winter of 1777-1778, families were asked to help replenish much needed provisions of the Revolutionary War soldiers, especially those at Valley Forge. The Thompson family responded with food, but Ruth also parted with "all the blankets, quilts & bedspreads in the house." Willing to do her share, she relinquished her labors of love and comfort for her family. She was remembered to have said, "We can make ourselves comfortable with wearing apparel till we make a new supply of bedding."[3] Her husband promised to give her the best materials when they became available after the War. In the late 1780s, James purchased for Ruth "a fine woolen dark blue in color."[4] Ruth made a wholecloth quilt and, using matching indigo thread, designed a floral medallion with outlines of twining vines of leaves and flowers. She then quilted parallel lines with

seven stitches to the inch, placed one-inch apart, to further emphasize the centerpiece. The pattern of the stitches is the enhancing element in a wholecloth quilt. Family history states that the backing fabric was made from wool raised on their Goshen farm.

Wholecloth, c. pre-1800, made by Ruth Benton Thompson (1742-1813), Goshen, calamanco, 92" x 85". Owned by the Henry Whitfield State Museum, Guilford, Connecticut.

Henry Whitfield House, c. 1639, Guilford. The oldest existing house in Connecticut and in New England.

Family history states that the quilt's backing fabric was made from wool raised on their farm.

15

Asenath Rising

The Rising name will always be associated with the Suffield area. The northwestern boundary lines between Connecticut and Massachusetts were disputed for nearly 150 years. The line did not stay straight but dipped south, leaving the town of Southwick in Massachusetts and an area known as the "Ponds" in Connecticut. This divot is known as "Rising Notch."

Asenath King was the fifth child born to John and Parnel Holcombe King around 1764/65 in Suffield. It was said that John was an educated man, and he held the Selectman's post in Suffield on multiple occasions. His large family was comprised of eight girls and one boy, John, the eldest, who drowned in the Agawam River.[1] James Rising, born on February 2, 1759, was also a Suffield native. His family owned significant land holdings along the Massachusetts border, known as "Rising Notch." James Rising was a soldier in the Revolutionary War.[2] The marriage date of James and Asenath is not known; however, the first of their five children was born in 1792.

Asenath made her indigo glazed quilt with its raised pineapple motif and feathered swag border in 1784 from wool and flax raised in Suffield—possibly in anticipation of her marriage to James. One can envision their romancing in the household's great room after the rest of the family had gone to bed; "Many of the first families in Connecticut can tell of such courtships." As unromantic as this may sound, the dye-tub used for the "blue" of the linsey-woolsey became the seat associated with the potential for romance. It was tucked away in the corner of the great fireplace, away from the watchful eye of a concerned father. Many a marriage was bravely proposed seated on the dye-tub hidden in those dark recesses of the eighteenth-century Connecticut homes.[3]

Calamanco, c. pre-1800, made by Asenath Rising (1764/65-1851), Suffield, wool, 87.25" x 93.25". *Courtesy of The Connecticut Historical Society. Acc #1601. Photo by David Stansbury.*

Catherine "Caty" Selleck

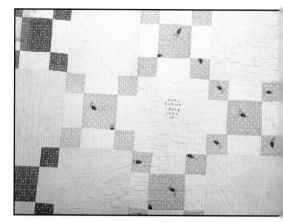

Nine-Patch is one of the earliest Connecticut quilt patterns, so it is not surprising that Darien's Caty Selleck chose to make it. This pattern was the earliest dated patchwork example documented by the Project. Caty Selleck's name and *"April 4, 1806"* are cross-stitched on the quilt.

Caty grew up on her father's extensive farm, called "The Farms" as their family still remembers it. Farms Road in Darien passes by their land holdings even today. From a young age, Caty became proficient in the necessary skills of spinning flax and wool, weaving the fibers into cloth, dying the cloth, and then fashioning the essentials for clothing for life in Connecticut during the early part of the nineteenth century. The family's memorial book contains this record:

> When {Caty} was 14 her father gave her all the fleece from a large flock of sheep. She worked with a will to get ready for the flax the next year. Then she was 15 years old – she was 14 with wool. That makes it 1797 and 15 years old with the flax 1798. She had to dye all the wool and get the dye from her father's wood. She must have worked with a good Selleck vim. She made beautiful towels, sheets, and pillow covers. All the feather beds and pillows were of linen – you shall have a piece. I got a feather bed. I change it carefully and save the linen liner. She made all her own dresses and coats, about the style they use now.[1]

Because of her great talent with cloth, it is believed that she took in spinning and weaving in order to support herself as an unmarried woman. Such women were called "spinsters," a designation that still applies to older, unmarried women, however, this was not to be Caty's fate.[2] In her late thirties she married her distant cousin, Kilbourne Selleck, and moved to his home in Salisbury. Fortunately, Caty signed and dated her quilt and recorded her place in Connecticut's quilt history.

Cross-stitched in the center of the quilt is *"Caty Selleck, April 4, 1806."*

THE SPINSTER.

Woodcut from *Scribner Monthly*, 1878. Many unmarried women of the late eighteenth century and early nineteenth century took in spinning and weaving to support themselves, hence the name "spinster" came into being.

Nine-Patch, April 4, 1806, made by Catherine (Caty) Selleck (b.1783), Darien, cotton, 90" x 88". Privately owned.

Betsey Smith Paine

Betsey Smith married John Paine on November 13, 1805. Her husband was a storeowner in West Woodstock. In 1808, the newly married couple moved to John's Aunt Anna Paine Chandler's homestead in the northeastern part of Woodstock. John was granted possession of the farm three years before his Aunt's death.[1]

With its gentle hills and gravelly-loomed soil, Woodstock was well suited to the grazing and cultivation of the land. Agriculture was its biggest industry. Domestic and household manufactures were the most labor-intensive activities of the time. In early nineteenth-century Woodstock, "Most of the primary and substantial fabrics of clothing are the products of domestic industry, there being a loom in almost every house."[2] Weaving cloth for the town's six mercantile stores in exchange for goods ranging from food to lumber kept the shuttles of Woodstock flying.[3] The village was watered by many small streams, including Muddy Brook, which flowed into the Quinebaug River. It was on the Muddy Brook that John joined with other incorporators to start the Muddy Brook Cotton Mfg. Co. in the north part of town. By 1819, it was said to have "large and commodious buildings."[4]

While John was serving as Justice of the Peace, Probate Judge, and a Representative to the Legislature, Betsey was bearing and raising the couple's eight children. It was after the birth of her first child, Samuel Chandler, that Betsey found time to make her indigo calamanco quilt. The stitches of

South view of the Congregational Church, Woodstock.

Woodcut from *History and Antiquities* by John Warner Barber, 1836.

the quilt etch a medallion artichoke design with parallel lines and feathered patterns. Her name and date, *"Betsey Paine, 1808"* are fixed in stitches on the glazed wool. The gold wool backing and wool filling certainly warmed her family through the cold northeastern Connecticut winters.

After twenty-one years of marriage, Betsey died on November 22, 1826. Two years later, John married her sister, Lucy Smith. Together, they did not have any children. Lucy was devoted to properly raising her sister's children and was remembered as a loving aunt and grandmother. Betsey, John, and Lucy are buried in that order in the East Woodstock Cemetery.

Along the top on the glazed wool is fixed in stitches *"Betsey Paine 1808." Photo by David Stansbury.*

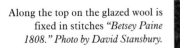

Wholecloth, 1808, made by Betsey Smith Paine (1783-1826), Woodstock, calamanco, 88" x 90". *Courtesy of The Connecticut Historical Society. Acc #1985.45.0. Photo by David Stansbury.*

Ann Ingersoll Brush

In anticipation of her marriage, Ann Ingersoll created this incredible, cutwork appliqué quilt in 1810. On November 23, 1812, Ann and Edward Brush became husband and wife. Similar to many New Englanders of the early nineteenth century, Edward believed his future economic success lay in the West. Around 1814, the newly married couple headed westward in their covered wagon to the territory of Indiana. Land records show purchases made in Laurel Township, Franklin County, on May 27, 1815 and March 22, 1816. Packed with care amongst the couple's belongings was Ann's beautiful wedding quilt.

During the next ten years, Ann was busy bearing and raising seven of her eight children in their farmhouse on a hill in Somerset, now Laurel, Indiana. Life was prosperous for this growing family. Writing to his father Benjamin, back in Greenwich, Connecticut, on Dec. 29, 1816, Edward invited his family to join him in "New Connecticut" where land cost but $1.25/acre. His oldest sister Fanny and her husband, William Rundle, did just that and became their neighbors.

Life and death went hand-in-hand in the nineteenth century and Ann was no stranger to the loss of precious life. She was four months pregnant with her eighth child and mourning the death of her seventh child when on August 10, 1825, Edward, while in Fort Wayne, Indiana, was stricken with typhoid fever and died at the age of thirty-four. The distance from Laurel to Fort Wayne was too great in 1825 to retrieve his remains, so the distressed family never knew where Edward was buried.

With her husband's sudden death, the financial repercussions were devastating for the widow and her family. After their land debts in Indiana were settled, Ann and her family were destitute. She returned to Connecticut with Fanny and William Rundle. The journey east took place sometime between August 1825 and January 1826. Crowded in that covered wagon were Uncle Rundle, Aunt Fanny, Ann, who was in her last trimester of pregnancy, Elma age eleven, Joseph Edward age nine, Shadrach age seven, Frances age five, Rebecca Ann age four, Mary Abigail age two, three Queen Anne style fiddle back chairs, and Ann's beloved quilt. Edward and Ann's eighth child, Samantha Reynolds, was born in Greenwich, January 18, 1826. Ann's economic plight forced her to ultimately disperse her children to various relatives to be raised, a painful decision many widows with small children were obliged to make. On September 2, 1828, however, Ann had all of the children baptized at the Stanwich Church.

Ann died on September 28, 1863 at the age of fifty and is buried in The Second Congregational Churchyard. The burial ground is near the Bush-Holley House of The Historical Society of the Town of Greenwich. Her legacy quilt is preserved in The Historical Society's collection and serves to remind us of the many Connecticut women who, with the hope of a bright future, followed their husbands' dreams in the westward movement.

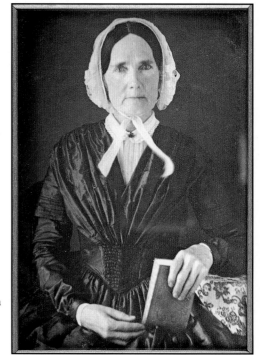

Ann Ingersoll Brush

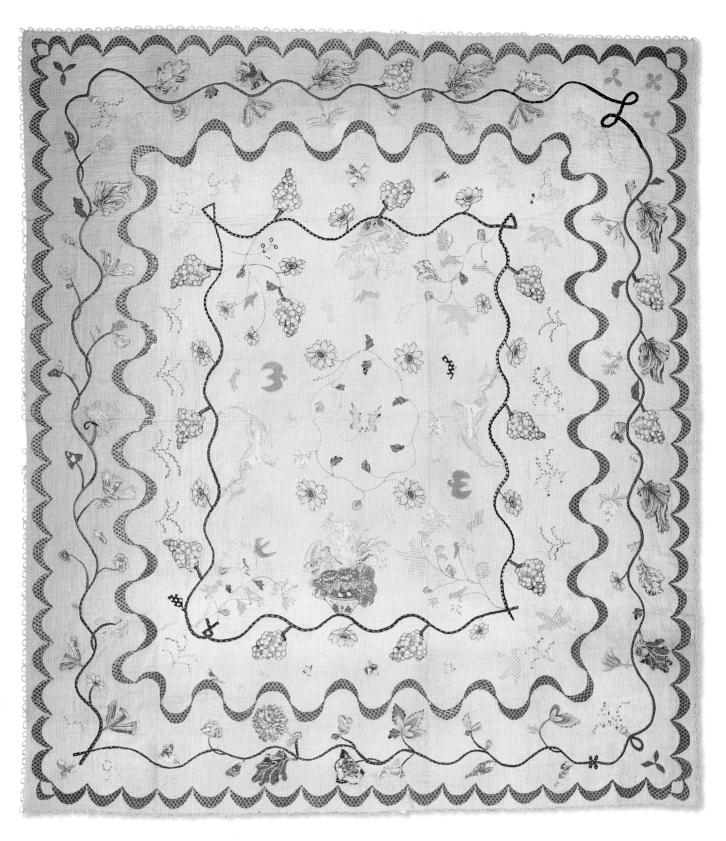

Medallion Appliqué, c. 1810, made by Ann Ingersoll Brush (1789-1863), Greenwich,
cotton, 85" x 97". Owned by The Historical Society of the Town of Greenwich.

The Jerusha Clark Peck Wedding Quilt and Sarah Pierce's Female Academy

Jerusha Clarke attended Miss Sarah Pierce's Female Academy in Litchfield around 1813. When Jerusha completed her education, she returned there to teach in 1816. Catharine Beecher, the daughter of Reverend Lyman Beecher, and her sister Harriet Beecher Stowe, were her contemporaries at the Academy.

Sarah Pierce supervised the education of more than three thousand young ladies and a few young men from across the United States and abroad. The most comprehensive list can be found in *To Ornament Their Minds: Sarah Pierce's Litchfield Female Academy 1792-1833*. It records 1,710 attendees, of those, 834 were from Connecticut, representing ninety-seven of its towns, and 876 were from other states and countries.[1]

Through Sarah Pierce's good example and continual encouragement, her students began to use their talents in sewing and quilting for the purpose of the better good and for the advancement of those less blest in life. Those who employed these skills benefited from gathering together to share the work, and quiltings and bees were commonplace in the first half of the nineteenth century.

Harriet Beecher Stowe, a Connecticut daughter, was a student at Miss Pierce's school when this quilt was made for Jerusha. That experience may have easily inspired her description of a quilting in her 1859 story, *The Minister's Wooing*:

> The quilting was in those days considered the most solemn and important recognition of a betrothal...When a wedding was forthcoming, there was a solemn review of the stories of beauty and utility thus provided, and the patchwork-spread best worthy of such distinction was chosen for the quilting. Thereto, duly summoned, trooped all intimate female friends of the bride, old and young; and the quilt being spread on a frame, and wadded with cotton, each vied with the others in the delicacy of the quilting she could put upon it. For the quilting was also a fine art, and had its delicacies and nice points—which grave elderly matrons discussed with judicious care. The quilting generally began at an early hour in the afternoon, and ended at dark with a great supper and general jubilee, at which that ignorant and incapable sex which could not quilt was allowed to appear and put in claims for consideration of another nature.[2]

Jerusha Phillips Clarke, born in March 1797, was from Northampton, Massachusetts, where her father operated a saddlery. On November 17, 1818, she wed Henry Peck of Berlin.[3] Henry was the son of Norman Peck, a sea captain of considerable wealth in the Merchant Marines.[4] In 1828, ten years after their marriage, Henry and Jerusha are listed as members of the First Church in New Haven.[5] Henry was a publisher at Dhurrie and Peck in New Haven, served as Mayor of New Haven, and as a State Representative from 1843 to 1848.[6] Their son, Horace, graduated from Yale in 1839. Jerusha died in 1887. Her beautiful Whig Rose quilt was returned to its place of origin in Litchfield and is among other archival records of Sarah Pierce's Female Academy.

Watercolor painting of The Litchfield Female Academy, c. 1827. Collection of the Litchfield Historical Society. Sarah Pierce's Litchfield Female Academy supervised the education of more than three thousand young women between 1792 and 1833.

View of the Litchfield Academy — *September 16th*

Whig Rose Variation, c. 1818, made by Students of The
Female Academy, Litchfield, cotton, 85" x 89". Owned by the
Litchfield Historical Society. *Photo by David Stansbury.*

Sarah "Sally" Plant Judson

The great elms at the foot of Academy Hill were planted in front of Sarah "Sally" Plant's house in 1804 when she was twenty-nine years old.[1] Sally was born on January 5, 1775, the second of four children of Solomon Plant and Sarah Bennett Plant.[2] The Plant's old saltbox homestead and Solomon's wheelwright shop were located at the corner of Broad and Elm Streets in Stratford. Solomon Plant produced spinning wheels at this location for more than fifty years. It was said that "all the spinning wheels in Fairfield County were either made or repaired here."[3] His business was profitable enough so that some of his children were able to attend the Stratford Academy. The Academy provided a classical education for boys and girls "whose lot was cast beneath the Stratford elms."[4]

Sally married Daniel Judson on September 10, 1797. They had eight children between 1800 and 1816. Sally outlived only three of her children, dying on August 14, 1857. She and Daniel are buried in the Congregational Burying Ground in Stratford.

The Sunburst quilt was made by Sally, c. 1830. It was quilted in a simple chevron pattern, and its size suggests that it was made as a gift for the birth of one of her grandchildren.

Sunburst, c. 1800-1840, made by Sarah "Sally" Plant Judson, Stratford, cotton, 51" x 56". Owned by Stratford Historical Society.

From Dress Cloth to Bed Cloth

This deep rose-colored, wholecloth quilt of calendered (a finishing process producing a flat, glossy, smooth surface by passing the fabric under pressure between a series of heated cylinders.)[1] wool or worsted began as a quilted petticoat in its first "life." Originally measuring eighty-six inches around with a length of thirty-four inches, it was sturdy enough to survive the centuries. Its beauty suggests that it was made or purchased for a special occasion. The color could have been achieved with the use of madder or cochineal dye. The lining of the petticoat, a coarse, homespun fabric, became the backing of the quilt.

Connecticut Yankee women, a most thrifty group, learned the wisdom and economic sensibilities of recycling centuries before its now-fashionable title. Not only did they make quilts from the leftover bits of new and worn fabric, but they also enshrined special items of clothing by giving them a place of honor in the center of a newly fashioned quilt.

Wholecloth, c. 1800-1840, maker unknown, worsted twill, 48" x 70". *Courtesy of The Connecticut Historical Society. Acc #1959.54.3. Photo by David Stansbury.*

Louisa Brigham

Connecticut families played an enormous role in the settlement of our entire nation. By the 1760s, Connecticut's adventurous responded to the need for cultivating new farming lands and for a more prosperous living. "Between 1780 and 1840 almost 750,000 people left Connecticut for greener pastures, some travelling north to western Massachusetts and Vermont, others west to New York, Pennsylvania, Ohio, Illinois and beyond…"[1] The family of Louisa Brigham was one of these families who migrated to Vermont during this time period.

The only memory of Louisa Brigham is her whimsical, light-hearted, early nineteenth-century appliqué "T" quilt. A cotton fringe finishes the single layer,

lightweight quilt. The colors of its prints have remained bright and cheery despite its 183 years. There is a twenty-inch drop at the foot of the quilt and twenty-two inch drops on each side. With the tiniest of cross-stitches sewn on her fabric legacy, she sealed her place in her family's history.

Louisa was born on April 9, 1793. She was twenty-five years of age when she signed and dated her quilt "L. B. 1818." Family history records that the quilt has been passed down through the females in the family. Eventually, it was brought back to Connecticut—the roots of Louisa's ancestral past. It has been in the safe keeping of the Foote family, Connecticut settlers since 1633.[2]

Louisa Brigham cross-stitched her initials *"L.B."* and *"1818"* in the center of her quilt.

Medallion Appliqué, 1818, Louisa Brigham (b. 1793), Barre, Vermont, cotton, 92.5" x 87". Owned by Lucy Foote Trudeau and L. Hamilton Foote. One can only imagine the inspiration for the appliquéd alligators.

Sarah Fish Lord and Lydia Lord

The common bond between Sarah Fish Lord and Lydia Lord was the Rev. Hezekiah Lord. A 1717 Yale College graduate, he became the minister of the Second Congregational Church of Preston around 1720. His first wife, Sarah Fish, whom he married in 1724, was from the coastal town of Groton.

Sarah was the youngest daughter of the seafaring Captain Fish. With the majority of Groton's men focused on the sea and fishing, the women were occupied at the loom. Domestic manufacturing of home and clothing textiles fully engaged the female industry of the time. It is said that "economy, simplicity, and plainness of life and manners" were their "cardinal, social and domestic virtues."[1]

Sarah embroidered a wool skirt with a worsted yarn in a floral design. She used multiple, fancy, crewel stitches to embellish and showcase her needlework skills. An occasion that might allow for a minister's wife to wear such a decorative item might have been an ordination ball, appropriate in some areas to welcome a new minister. Or she may have fashioned it for her wedding dress.

Sarah's life was short, as she died only nine years after becoming a wife and mother. Left behind with his four children, Reverend Lord married his second wife, Zeviah Backus. The eldest of their children, Nathaniel, was to become the father of Lydia Lord, born in 1787. As the eldest son, Nathaniel most likely acquired the bulk of his parents' estate and belongings, including Sarah's embroidered wool skirt which had been stored away for over fifty years. In the use-up and make-do fashion of a true Connecticut Yankee, Lydia used the wool skirt as the center of her quilt and surrounded it with a brown wool border on three sides. Backed and batted with wool, Lydia's decorative additions are the ornate quilting patterns of feathers, pineapples, and parallel lines.

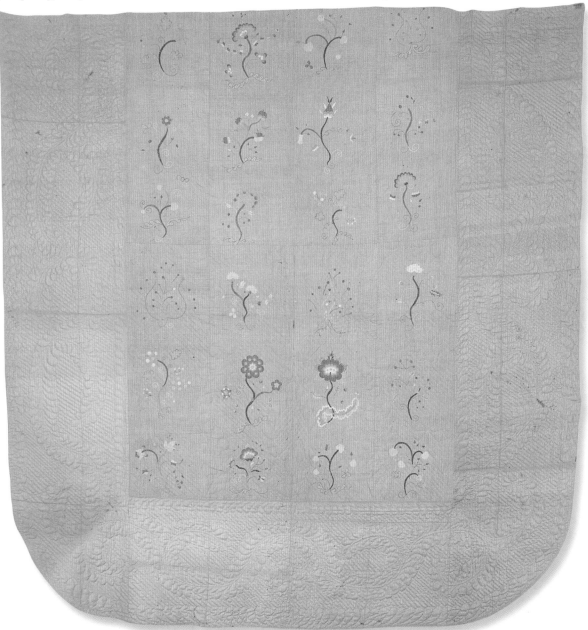

Embroidered Medallion, c. 1820, made by Lydia Lord (1787-1829), Preston, wool, 94" x 95.5". Owned by New Haven Colony Historical Society. *Photo by David Stansbury.*

Sarah Edmond Booth's Wedding Quilt

As a country doctor's wife and the daughter of an honorable judge and member of Congress, Sarah Edmond Booth did not lack for worldly possessions and the gentler comforts of life. Her wedding quilt seen here was unused and kept in the best condition. Made in 1820, this white cotton, wholecloth quilt is enriched with many quilting designs, stuffed work, and cording. The sunflower medallion design is surrounded by triple diamond grid quilting, feathered circles, and parallel lines, and it was one of the few white-on-white quilts documented by the Project.

Sarah Edmond and Cyrenius Booth were raised by two prominent families in Newtown in the early 1800s. This farming community situated in the west central section of the state was populated with more sheep than people throughout the nineteenth century. Over four thousand sheep grazed in the pastures and fields of Newtown in 1800. At that time the cost of one sheep was seventy-five cents. They were so valued that they were declared "free commoners" and could pasture anywhere.[1] Individual farmers maintained herds, and the town kept a large flock of sheep and hired a town shepherd. The "Ram Pasture," a poundage for sheep, is still present in Newtown's center and remains as an historic landmark of a time gone by.[2]

Sarah, the second child, was born on June 24, 1800 to William and Elizabeth Edmond.[3] Cyrenius was born in the same town three years before Sarah. As childhood acquaintances, it is possible that they attended the same school and church since their prominent families shared the same social circles. Cyrenius is fondly remembered in Newtown's history as the country doctor, tending to the ills of the Newtown families for half a century. Large, gracious, white houses line the wide main thoroughfare of Newtown where Sarah and Cyrenius Booth grew up. Representing two of the family's legacies are The Booth Memorial Library and Edmond Town Hall on Main Street.

Sarah Edmond Booth

Wholecloth, 1820, made by Sarah Edmond Booth, Newtown, cotton,
84" x 90.5". Owned by The Cyrenius H. Booth Library.

Fanny Bolles Bill Hurlbutt

Late summer was giving way to autumn when Fanny Bolles Bill was born on September 26, 1792 in Groton. She was the daughter of Benjamin Bill III and Amy Bolles Bill, who had been married the previous year. Fanny's father had been wounded while serving in the State Militia in the Battle of Groton Heights, Sept. 6, 1781, and received a stipend of $8 a year from the U.S. government. Perhaps he was seeking a greater fortune, or the lure of the sea drew him, but he set sail for the West Indies in January of 1795 and was never heard from again. Fanny was only two years old.

On February 3, 1822 Fanny married Peter Lester Hurlbutt, son of Rufus Hurlbutt and Hannah Lester. They had four children before Peter died during the winter of 1837. It is presumed that she made this quilt sometime during her marriage, and she bequeathed her unused quilt to her granddaughter and namesake, Fanny Bill Hurlbutt (daughter of John Hurlbutt and Abby Jane Bailey), who was born sixteen days prior to Fanny's death.

Fanny Bill Hurlbutt never married, but lived with her parents and cared for her mother after her father died. Upon her mother's death in 1906, she began a career in nursing. As is often the case, talent transcended time, and Fanny Bill Hurlbutt was also a skilled needlewoman. When she passed away in 1952, she continued the tradition of passing along the original Fanny's quilt with the stipulation that it never be used, and that it always descend to a female member of the family. The current owner will pass it along to her only daughter, who will have the unenviable task of deciding which granddaughter will someday inherit this lovely legacy.

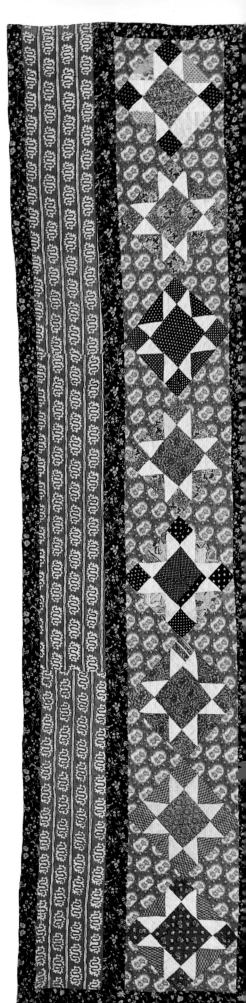

Variable Star Strippy, c. 1822, made by Fanny Bolles Bill Hurlbutt (1792-1866), Groton, cotton, 89" x 93". Owned by Belle Robinson.

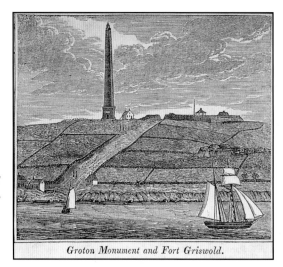

Fanny Bolles Bill Hurlbutt

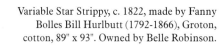

Woodcut from *History and Antiquities* by John Warner Barber, 1836.

Groton Monument and Fort Griswold.

Mabel Ruggles Canfield and Elizabeth Canfield Tallmadge

*I*n the course of documenting Connecticut quilts, a number of quilts were found to have been produced by the combined efforts of several generations. In some cases, it was the actual course of construction that benefited from this involvement; in other instances it was the sharing of carefully saved fabrics from one family member to the next. Recycling materials was a very common practice, even among wealthier families. The Litchfield Historical Society's "Constitution Quilt," as it has become known, made by mother and daughter, is just one example of the hands and hearts of several family members joining together.

Mabel Ruggles, one of thirteen children of prosperous New Milford residents, Captain Lazarus Ruggles and Hannah Bostwick Ruggles, was born in 1760. She married Judson Canfield, a Yale graduate and lawyer, and moved to Sharon in 1786.

Mabel and Judson's daughter, Elizabeth Canfield, was born in 1793, and along with her sister, Julia, was educated at the renowned Litchfield Female Academy, a bastion of educational and artistic skills enjoyed by genteel young ladies of the day. Nearby was Tapping Reeve's Litchfield Law School, where the young men in attendance were quick to note Elizabeth's exceptional beauty, dubbing her the "Rose of Sharon." On May 22, 1815, she married one of the law school's graduates, Frederick Augustus Tallmadge, son of Revolutionary War hero and prominent local merchant Col. Benjamin Tallmadge, Sr.

All of the materials in this quilt are English block prints, c. 1790-1810. The calico with rosebuds print is from dresses belonging to Elizabeth and her sister, c. 1810. Presumably, these dresses held special memories for the girls as their inclusion was specified in paperwork accompanying the quilt. It is, however, the predominant fabric, the off-white background trellis pattern with roses in different shades of brown, that gives this quilt its name. It is recorded that this particular fabric had been the stateroom curtains of Lt. Benjamin Tallmadge (1792-1831) while he was on duty aboard the USS Constitution. During his service, the Constitution was in the Mediterranean Sea to protect American commerce. Lt. Tallmadge died at sea near Gibraltar on June 20, 1831. Although he never married, as Elizabeth's brother-in-law, he may have sent her the rose fabric, recalling her "Rose of Sharon" nickname, or as a souvenir of his travels. Consequently, two fabrics that started out oceans apart—the dresses and the curtains—were united in the hands and hearts of a mother-daughter team.

The Constitution Quilt, c. 1800-1840, made by Mabel Ruggles Canfield (b.1760) and Elizabeth Canfield Tallmadge (1793-1875), Litchfield, cotton and linen, 84" x 91". Owned by the Litchfield Historical Society. This quilt gets its name from the fabric on the outside border. The off-white cloth with its brown roses had been used as stateroom curtains aboard the USS Constitution. *Photo by David Stansbury.*

Stylized palm trees and floral sprays direct your eye to the center of the quilt. *Photo by David Stansbury.*

The Charter Oak

O ne of the earliest, most time-honored stories in Connecticut's history surrounds The Charter Oak. Indians were Connecticut's first settlers. They pleaded with the white faces that came from strange lands to revere the tall, white oak (Quercus alba) that had become their tribal landmark:

> *It has been the guide of our ancestors for hundreds of years, as to the time of planting corn, when the leaves are the size of a mouse's ear, then is the time to put the seed into the ground.*[1]

Connecticut's first Constitution was hidden from the British within the great recesses of the ancient oak. With that single incident, Connecticut acquired two of its current nicknames: The Constitution State and The Charter Oak State.

The Charter Oak grew on a rise near Hartford's Main Street near the home of the Wyllys family. In 1805, it was written about the tree:

> *That venerable tree, which concealed the charter of our rights, stands at the foot of Wyllys hill. The first inhabitants of that town found it standing in the height of its glory. Age seems to have curtailed its branches, yet it is not exceeded in the height of its coloring, or the richness of its foliage. The trunk measures twenty-one feet in circumference, and near seven in diameter. The cavity, which was the asylum of our charter, was near the roots, and large enough to admit a small child. Within the space of eight years, that cavity closed, as if it had fulfilled its divine purpose for which it had been reared.*[2]

Acorn and oak leaf jewelry made of wood from the original Charter Oak Tree, c. 1860.

Controversy surrounded the age of the tree. In the mid nineteenth century, estimates ranged from 600 to 2,000 years of age. At its base, the diameter was fourteen feet. At four feet above the ground, the diameter was nine feet and thirty-three feet around.[3] On August 21, 1856, a windstorm caused the tree to topple. Bells throughout the state tolled in mourning and bands played funeral marches for The Charter Oak.

The fame of The Charter Oak has been immortalized since the beginning of the nineteenth century. It was celebrated with a dance called the Charter Oak Reel. After its demise, its limbs were used to construct chairs for the governor and mayor, and also made into pianos and other memorabilia.[4] Quilt appliqué patterns of oak leaves, oak and reel, oak tree silhouettes, and acorns were popularly made to pay special homage to the qualities of freedom and independence, and to symbolize long life.[5]

The Charter Oak by Charles DeWolf Brownell. *Courtesy of The Connecticut Historical Society.*

Oak Leaf and Reel, c. 1800-1840, Gift of the Booth Family, New
Milford, cotton, 78" x 84". Owned by New Milford Historical Society.

The Hollister Family Chintz Quilt

The nineteenth-century *Reminiscences of Mrs. Swift* of Winchester left this touching account as to the value of Diana Avered's beautiful eighteenth-century, chintz cloth:

> *During the war my Aunt Diana, one Monday morning, received an invitation to a wedding just one week from that evening; she must, therefore, have a 'new gown.' The only store in the town was south of the burying-ground, near Torrington line, nearly four miles distant. My grandmother rode over the hills to the store, where she found a pattern of chintz which she could have for eleven and a half yards of checked woolen shirting for soldiers' wear: but could not buy it with 'Continental bills.' The old lady returned about one hour before 'sundown' and told her story. 'We had,' says my aunt, 'wool, cards, wheel, net, loom, and blue dye all in the house, but not a thread of yarn. That night, before I went to bed, I carded, spun, washed, and put into the dye-tub one run of yarn, and so the work went on; the cloth was wove, the 'gown' pattern purchased, made up, and worn to the wedding at the week's end. I have often seen this gown; and in 1843 I slept under a bed-quilt, made principally from its remains, in a good state of preservation.[1]*

This story could have easily accompanied the Hollister family quilt. In her book, *Coming of Age; Four Centuries of Connecticut Women and Their Choices*, author Ruth Barnes Moynihan wrote, "A bride's gown, past or present, was likely to be the most beautiful piece of clothing she owned. The needlework and the fabric (not necessarily white until the late nineteenth and twentieth centuries) were a testimony to both her love and her talent, especially if she made it herself. And the gown became an heirloom, to be preserved or perhaps remade by daughter and granddaughter."[2] The provenance of some other quilts documented by the Project record that they had been made from fabric of a special dress or wedding gown.

The Hollister family first came to Wethersfield in the early seventeenth century. It was another one hundred years before they settled in Washington. The nineteenth-century Washington Hollisters represented families ranging from the families of a U.S. Senator, writer, and poet, the famous Gideon Hollister, to the Franklin Hollisters, farmers and local laborers of the town.[3] After reading Diana Avered's story, it is easy to imagine the fabric was the remains of the fancy dresses or wedding gowns of Hollister women, reused to create this stunning quilt.

Unfortunately, when the quilt was donated to the Gunn Museum of Washington, the only provenance provided was that it was made from chintz purchased at the local dry goods store. In the quilt's construction, the collection of chintz fabrics was cut in large squares set on-point and used in border triangles, thus keeping the pattern of the prints intact as much as possible. This quilt has been maintained in near pristine condition with the glazed finish or sheen of the chintz still present. The medley pleasantly blends the soft florals to achieve a medallion effect.

Chintz One-Patch, c. 1820-1840, made by the Hollister Family,
cotton, 65" x 87". Owned by Gunn Historical Museum.

Opposite page:
Sampler of chintz fabrics used in the quilt.

Clarinda Beers McKay

This patriotic, imported fabric, featuring our first few Presidents, came to America from France. It was made specifically for exportation to America around 1830 and was roller printed in a blue, brown, or pink toile. This presidential quilt is attributed to Clarinda Beers McKay, born on October 4, 1833.

The light blue and white toile depicts our first six Presidents and their dates in office: Washington, Adams, Jefferson, Madison, Monroe, John Q. Adams, and Andrew Jackson. Jackson, just elected to office, was featured in the center of the panel encircled with the words *"President of the United States from March 4, 1829 to ____. Supreme Commander of the Army & Navy."* Underneath Jackson's image is *"Magnani-*

mous in Peace, Victorious in War." Frigates and eagles carrying *E Pluribus Unum* banners in their beaks surround the Presidents.

Clarinda Beers was only an infant when this fabric first appeared in the United States as a French import, and it is possible that the quilt was made for her birth. Its relatively unused condition indicates that it might have been stored away by her mother who recognized its commemorative value. Clarinda was married at the young age of fifteen on January 13, 1848 to Samuel McKay. It is uncertain where Clarinda lived throughout her eighty years, but both she and her husband are buried in the Great Plain Cemetery in Danbury.[1]

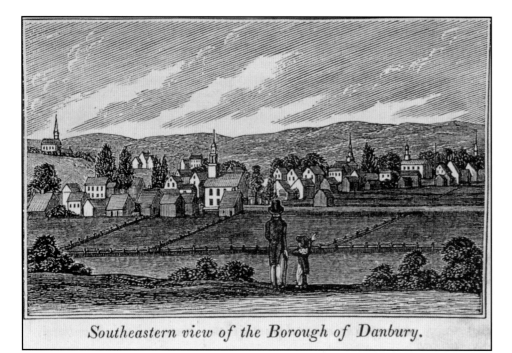

Southeastern view of the Borough of Danbury.

Woodcut from *History and Antiquities* by John Warner Barber, 1836.

President's Quilt, c. 1800-1840, attributed to Clarinda Beers McKay (1833-1907),
Danbury, cotton, 67" x 57". Owned by Wynne McKay Marschalk.

Content Newton

Content Newton of Durham is credited with this sizeable pieced quilt that is a study in indigo resist and discharge printed fabric. Her ancestors came to Durham in 1724 to the Haddam Quarter section of the town. Roger Newton was the first ancestor to come to Connecticut with Thomas Hooker in 1636.

Content is noted in her family's genealogical records for her fine needlework and sewing. Many artifacts of her work have passed down through the generations. It was said that "she did much of the weaving, sitting at the loom whole days. It stood in the east chamber, with the window towards the sunrise. This provision was a work of time, and was always begun early in every well-to-do New England family."[1] When her sister, Parnel, married in 1814, she had two dozen flax linen sheets in her chest, made from flax raised on the farm and spun and woven by her sister.

Content had become engaged to a Mr. Pearce. In August 1813, at the age of twenty-four, she received this note from her betrothed, who was in failing health:

> *Even I, the lowest of the throng.*
> *Unskild in verse of artful Song*
> *Shall shortly shroud my humble head,*
> *And mix with them, among the dead.*[2]

Her fiancée recovered and went on to marry another. Unimpaired by this rejection and the turn of events in her life, Content pursued her love of dance. This was a popular recreation for the young people in the Commonwealth of Connecticut. "The people learned good manners, first from the district schools, secondly from public worship, thirdly from military service, and fourthly from dancing."[3] At the family's church, the Congregational minister, Reverend David Smith, had from the pulpit just preached of the deleterious effects of balls. Attending such events would be looked upon as promoting vice and as being opposed to piety. Disobeying her father, she met a gentleman at a friend's house for the opportunity to go to a ball. Content was the only one of her family who did not join the church. It was said that her life never flourished again.

Content remained unmarried, living in the family farmhouse. In 1831, on her way to visit her sister Parnel, her horse and carriage went out of control on a steep hill. She sustained a fall that broke her wrist and leg. Her nephew, Henry Huntington Newton (1840-1907), recalls in his memoirs that Aunt Content had to receive hypos.[4] Crippled by her accident, she must have remained in pain until her death in 1859.

This early blue and white quilt is just one of many nineteenth-century quilts discovered in the attic after her death. There are over twenty-five different indigo resist and discharge prints on fine and coarse fabrics incorporated into this quilt. The white fabric in the quilt and on the backing is a plain cotton muslin and may have been woven by Content. The allover pieced design is set off with a streak of lightning or zigzag border common to many nineteenth-century quilts with Connecticut provenance. It is simply quilted with two circles in the white alternate blocks and around the borders.

Wonderful selection of indigo prints, c. 1830.

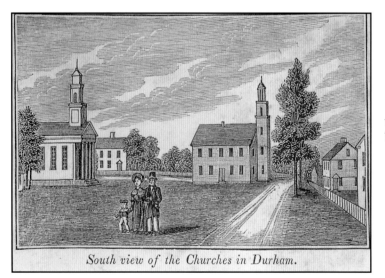

Woodcut from *History and Antiquities* by John Warner Barber, 1836.

Young Man's Fancy, c. 1830, made by Content Newton (1789-1859),
Durham, cotton, 94" x 98". Owned by Sue Reich.

Henrietta Frances Edwards Whitney

"At least, we know our Edwards women fair
Have, by their marriages, brought talent rare,
And such as well may call out all our pride
Into the line to which they are allied."[1]

Henrietta Frances Edwards lived a life of privilege even before her marriage to Eli Whitney, the inventor of the cotton gin. She was born on June 28, 1786 in New Haven to the Honorable Pierpoint Edwards and his wife, Frances Ogden Edwards of Bridgeport, and was the eighth of their eleven children.

Henrietta was thirty-one and Eli was fifty-six when they married in New Haven in January 1817. Twenty-five years earlier, in 1792, Eli had invented the cotton gin while living at Mulberry Grove in Savannah, Georgia. It resulted in a rise in cotton exportation from 189,000 pounds in 1791 to 41,000,000 pounds in 1803. There were so many infringements upon his cotton gin patent that it took sixty lawsuits before Eli received settlement. Known in his family as an "inventor of moving parts of iron and steel," he turned his attention to the manufacture of arms. A village in New Haven called Whitneyville was the upshot of the armory production.

The New Haven known to Henrietta was the largest city in Connecticut, with a population of a little over seven thousand, pleasant streets, charming squares, and a very spacious green. It was also noted for its harbor, its markets, and its roads. *The Fulton*, the first steamboat from New York, made two round trips per week. The price for passage was $5.00.[2] As one of Connecticut's "connecting" towns, New Haven's roads radiated like wheel spokes to New York, New Milford, Woodbury, Litchfield, Hartford, Farmington, Middletown, Norwich, and Saybrook.

Eli and Henrietta had three daughters and a son during their life together. By 1825, only eight short years after their marriage, Henrietta laid her husband to rest in New Haven's Grove Street Cemetery. The epitaph she chose for his tomb reads:

"Eli Whitney, the inventor of the Cotton Gin. Of useful Science and Arts,
the efficient patron and improver. Born Dec'r 8th, 1765
Died Jan 8th, 1825.
In social relations of life, a model of excellence.
With private affection weeps at his tomb, his country honors his memory."[3]

Besides the death of her husband, Henrietta suffered the heartache and loss of two other loved ones between 1823 and 1826. Her youngest daughter, Susan Edwards, died at the age of twenty-one months and her father, Pierpoint, died in 1826. In addition to raising her three remaining children, Henrietta was left with the responsibility for her husband's businesses until her own son could assume control. It was after Eli Whitney, Jr. graduated from Princeton in 1841 that he managed the manufacturing concerns of the family. It was for Henrietta's granddaughter Susan Huntington Whitney, born August 1, 1849, the daughter of her only son, that this pristine quilt was created.

South view of Whitneyville, in Hamden.

Woodcut from *History and Antiquities* by John Warner Barber, 1836.

The pattern of the pieced diamond and square is as difficult to draft as it is to piece. With the same floral design centered in each square, this quilt was not haphazardly made. It possesses a serene beauty and has retained its sheen for over 150 years. *Photo by David Stansbury.*

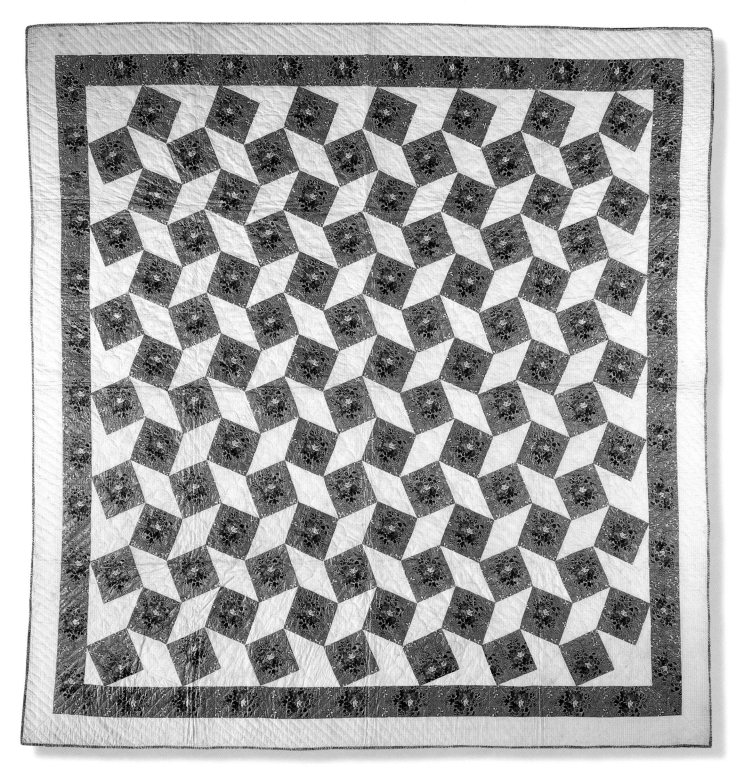

Two-Patch, 1849, made by Henrietta Frances Edwards Whitney (1786-1870), New Haven, cotton, 85" x 87.5". Owned by New Haven Colony Historical Society. *Photo by David Stansbury.*

The First Independent Universalist Church — Hartford

The First Independent Universalist Church was still in its infancy when the women of the congregation made this quilt. The Reverend Henry Birdsall Soule was the minister from 1846 to 1850. His diary records a glimpse of his life: "Fifteen afternoons have my wife and myself spent in calling upon our parishioners; and yet we have not got round, Poor Caroline is worn out."[1] The church records detail 128 funerals during this time; it is possible this memorial quilt was made to honor one of his deceased parishioners. Reverend Soule's wife, *"Mrs. Caroline A.*

Soule – 1847" is one of the thirty-one signatures that appear on the quilt.

In 1846, the Universalist Female Relief Society of the church had just been renamed the Universalist Social Benevolent Society. Their work was focused on sewing meetings and fairs. They performed charitable works to support members of their church.[2]

King David's Crown is an uncommon pattern to be used in a signature quilt. It's unusual use, however, is typical of Connecticut's signature quilts. Of the 3,000 plus quilts documented by The Connecti-

cut Quilt Search Project, there were 129 signature quilts. Sixty-five were quilts with many Connecticut towns listed or quilts with strong Connecticut provenance. Stylistically, Connecticut favored the Album/Chimneysweep pattern; however, fifty-four signed and dated quilts were made in other patterns.

King David's Crown, March 17, 1848, made by members of The First Independent Universalist Church, Hartford, 91" x 92", cotton. Owned by The Universalist Church of West Hartford.

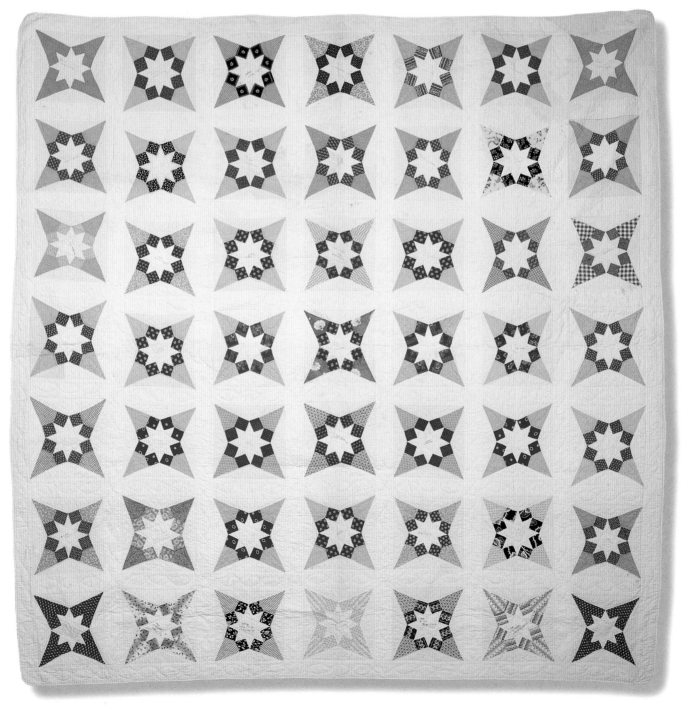

Chips & Whetstones, 1846-1847, made by Sarah Ann Weaver Newcomb (1825-1914), New London, cotton, 86.5" x 101". Owned by Jennifer Lattin Julier. Sarah Ann, who made this quilt for her wedding, wrote in her autobiography, *"It was not the custom of parents then as now to announce the engagement of their daughters, but frequent allusion to it caused me many painful blushes."*

Sarah Ann Weaver Newcomb

Eliza Jane Bishop Judson

Halfway along Weekeepeemee Road, on the country road that leads from Bethlehem to Woodbury, is a substantial, Georgian style farmhouse built on a granite foundation around 1800. As newlyweds in 1851, Harmon and Eliza Judson purchased this house in the Litchfield Hills with its outbuildings and vast land holdings for their first and only home.[1] Many members of the Judson family lived up and down this road, also known as a "shunpike," which was built by local people to avoid paying tolls on the road to Washington.

Eliza was the youngest of three children, and the only daughter born to Leman and Dotha D. Bishop on April 4, 1833. Both of her parents were from Bethlem (later changed to Bethlehem), a Connecticut village just a stone's throw from the farmlands on Weekeepeemee. Eliza's grandparents lived on Carmel Hill Road just east in Bethlem. Harmon Judson was one of the young farmers renting property from the Bishop's extensive land holdings before his 1851 marriage to Eliza.[2]

According to family lore, at the age of sixteen and in anticipation of her marriage to Harmon, Eliza made her Album signature quilt between 1849 and 1850 at a time when the population of Woodbury was 1,484.[3] Made possibly as an engagement quilt, it was signed by members of her family and friends. This quilt is undoubtedly one of the finest signature quilts in the Album pattern documented by the Connecticut Quilt Search Project. Set straight in an orderly design, its blocks are separated with triple sashing and corner blocks. The colors of its prints are still ever so vibrant. In keeping with several nineteenth-century Connecticut quilts, it is framed with a zigzag border.

Through each generation, Eliza's quilt has been passed down to a female in the family at the age of sixteen. Her betrothal heirloom was given to her daughter, Emma Mary Judson Thompson, who lived in Waterbury after her marriage. Emma's daughter, Gertie Emma Thompson Candee, born April 27, 1878, owned the quilt next. Esther Miriam Candee Beach, born May 29, 1910, was the last owner. After moving to Arizona in 1975, she returned it to the Old Bethlem Historical Society in the village of Bethlehem.[4]

Eliza Jane Bishop signed the quilt before her 1851 marriage to Harmon Judson.

Album Quilt, c. 1849, made by Eliza Jane Bishop Judson (1833-1912), Old
Bethlem, cotton, 82" x 94". Owned by The Old Bethlem Historical Society.

47

Esther Scofield Sands

Esther Scofield was born January 4, 1820 in Darien, one of nine children of Ezra Scofield, a sixth generation New Englander, and Elizabeth Clock Scofield. Although little is known of her early years, they may have been turbulent ones, for in 1832 the Probate Court appointed her oldest brother, William Rufus Scofield, as guardian of Esther and her siblings.

An unusual move for the times, the court's motivation is unclear, but it was decided that Ezra was "not a suitable person" to be in charge of his children.[1] There is also mention of a will probated in November of 1831 leaving the property of his father-in-law to Elizabeth, and subsequently her children, adding more mystery to their domestic situation. Whatever the court's motivation, William Rufus also received title to the family homestead, the Bates-Scofield house, while Ezra and his wife are reported to have relocated to his mother's home at the Scofield Inn. Esther remained in her brother's care until Dr. Samuel Sands came into her life.

On June 2, 1853, Esther married the kindly and highly respected doctor, who soon purchased the Bates-Scofield house. Both of their children were born there, and the Sands' lived a generous and benevolent life from beneath its rafters. Their only surviving child, Mary Katherine, grew to womanhood there.

It may have been while Esther was still living with her brother that she made her Eight-Point Radiating Star quilt with appliquéd oak leaves, perhaps in preparation for her upcoming wedding. It is signed in cross-stitch, *"E.A. Scofield, Darien, Conn 1850."*

Esther's legacy is multifaceted. Not only does her family home now house The Darien Historical Society—and once again her quilt—but many years later scraps left over from this delightful quilt created a legacy of their own in a quilt made by Esther's daughter, Mary Katherine Sands Bibbins.

Esther with daughter, Mary Katherine, c. 1900.

The corner is folded over to display the cross-stitched name of *"E.A. Scofield, Darien, Conn 1850."*

Prairie Stars, 1850, made by Esther Scofield Sands, (1820-1911), Darien, cotton, 93" x 96". *From the collection of and courtesy of The Darien Historical Society. All Rights Reserved.*

Mary Katherine Sands Bibbins

Born the daughter of well-to-do parents, Dr. Samuel Sands and Esther Scofield Sands, Mary Katherine Sands spent her early years immersed in the fine studies available to ladies of the day. It was obvious that her family's household was a genteel one, for in her father's obituary it states that he was "large hearted and benevolent…" and "possessed that gentleness which is characteristic of a good man…"[1] Taking advantage of her opportunities, Mary Katherine went on to become a fine artist and a respected art instructor.

Perhaps her early artistic talents were invoked in needlework, for her Sunbursts quilt was made while she was still a single woman living in her mother's household and utilized her mother's fabric scraps. This particular quilt shows a high level of graphic skill and fine needlework, a striking companion to the quilt made by her mother, Esther Scofield Sands.

On June 24, 1894, Mary Katherine married Arthur Silliman Bibbins, principal of the Darien Center School. They remained in her family homestead, where they raised their only child, Arthur Sands Bibbins, who in later years brought his own wife to live in the family homestead. Along with this quilt, portraits of Mary Katherine and her mother, plus paintings by Mary Katherine (including one of the family homestead) are displayed in the Darien Museum and Historical Society: a lasting tribute to two talented Connecticut women.

Mary Katherine Sands Bibbins, c. 1895.

Mary Katherine made her quilt prior to her 1894 marriage. The corner of the quilt is folded over to show the pretty fabric backing.

Sunbursts in a Garden Maze, c. 1865-1890, made by Mary Katherine Sands Bibbins, (1854-1931), Darien, cotton, 83" x 83". *From the collection of and courtesy of The Darien Historical Society. All Rights Reserved.*

Sunburst, 1839, made by Jane Esther St. John Raymond, Wilton, cotton, 87" x 104". Owned by the Danbury Museum and Historical Society. Jane Esther St. John was born in 1812 in Wilton. She was one of six children of Bella St. John and Jane (Keeler) St. John. On June 4, 1839 she married Cyrus E. Raymond and they were the parents of two daughters. Jane made the Sunburst quilt as a wedding quilt in 1839. The outstanding border is appliquéd with vines, leaves, artichokes, birds, and flowers. The quilt is in very good condition, and was donated to the Danbury Historical Society in 1989 by the great-great-granddaughter of the quiltmaker.

Tulip Variation with Maple Leaf, c. 1840-1865, made by Harriet Evaline Wiard Bevans, Wolcott, cotton, 83" x 84". Owned by Leelaine Picker. Harriet was an experienced needlewoman who taught her son, Walter, to sew, knit, crochet, and quilt. This quilt was a gift made for him. The swag and tassel border is a perfect complement to the 12" blocks set on point. The sharp edges of the appliqué are sewn with black and white threads. The quilting is ten stitches to the inch and it has a woven tape binding.

Harriet Evaline Wiard Bevans

"...the ubiquitous and superabounding Meads."[1]

The Mead Quilts from Fairfield County

Two quilts, one from southern and the other from northern Fairfield County, reunite the Mead family, whose original ancestors came to Connecticut two centuries earlier. It all began with William Mead, who traveled from England on the ship *Elizabeth* in April 1635. Making his way to Fairfield County via Wethersfield, he finally established himself there in 1641. It was from William Mead's two sons, John and Joseph, that the Mead families of Fairfield County sprung. John was the paternal ancestor of the Greenwich Meads, and his brother, Joseph, was the progenitor of the Norwalk, Ridgefield, and northern Fairfield County Meads.[2]

The Mead signature quilt in the Chimneysweep/Album pattern is dated 1851, and is the most common pattern found in signature quilts in Connecticut. The forty-nine blocks on the quilt have multiple signatures. A block in the corner of the quilt states *"Finished May 1852."* One hundred and four signatures of Mead family women are represented on this quilt. Mead women were dedicated to the multitude of social, educational, spiritual, and civic concerns of nineteenth-century Greenwich.

Album, c. 1853, made by the Mead Family, Ridgefield, cotton, 96" x 97". Owned by The Keeler Tavern Preservation Society, Inc. One of the greatest concentrations of Meads was in Ridgefield. They were descendants of the Joseph Mead line, settling in northern Fairfield County. Ridgefield's Main Street today is still bordered by large elegant houses, and crowning the approach to the center of town is The Keeler Tavern. Dating from the Revolutionary War, it became the chief stopping place of weary travelers. Today it houses the historical collection of the town of Ridgefield. The names of twenty-five Meads, nine Keelers, three Seeleys, and two Tompkins are all scribed on the quilt in the same hand.

Album, c. 1851, made by the Mead Family, Greenwich, cotton, 96" x 97". Owned by The Historical Society of the Town of Greenwich.

55

The Zachariah Ferris Quilt

This appliquéd and pieced Sampler has thirty-six blocks and tells the story of the descendants of one of the founding families of New Milford. The lives and deaths of forty-one family members from three generations are depicted in the blocks and some of the blocks have multiple names. An entire book could be devoted to the Ferris family, their fabric legacy, and their contributions to Connecticut's history.

The first Zachariah Ferris came to New Milford around 1706 through Charlestown, Massachusetts, and Stratford, Connecticut. His daughter, Sarah, was the first white child to be born in New Milford in 1710.[1] Zachariah, a surveyor and prominent man of New Milford, was a member of the First Church, the Congregational Meetinghouse, which he helped to build. His family, however, became affiliated with Connecticut's first Quaker Church, like many New Englanders responding to the religious revival of the 1730s through the 1750s. The Quaker Church cemetery in New Milford was plotted out by Zachariah, and the graves of many of his descendants, whose names appear on this quilt, can be seen there.

Nearly one hundred years after Zachariah Ferris settled in New Milford, his descendant, the fifth generation Zachariah Ferris, married Hannah Marsh on September 15, 1802. Together, they lived on his father's homestead on Rocky River; an area also known as Jerusalem, now buried beneath Candlewood Lake. The local lore of New Milford had always attributed this quilt to Zachariah, the founding father. Research shows that it was the family of Zachariah and Hannah Marsh Ferris whose lives are memorialized on the quilt.

At the center of the quilt, Zachariah, the patriarch, is depicted: *"Zachariah Ferris Age 75."* He is symbolized as a stately oak tree in the winter season of its life. Wife Hannah's block is to his right on the quilt and reads *"Hannah Ferris Age 69."* The continuous wreath of ivy encircles an anchor with the word *Hope* above it. Spreading out from the blocks representing Zachariah and Hannah are those depicting their ten children, their spouses, grandchildren, and great-grandchildren. All their children lived into adulthood, except for Eunice Cordelia, who was born when her mother was forty-two and her father forty-nine. Her brief life lasted but two and a half years for she died in October 1829 after eating poisonous berries.[2] She is depicted as one of the rosebuds with *"Eunice Cordelia Ferris"* and accompanied by a touching poem of the family's children lost to an early death.

The seventh child of Zachariah and Hannah, Abby Jane, was born on May 21, 1819. Her block, a most beautiful appliqué floral bouquet, is inscribed with *"Abby Jane Haviland Age 34."* *"Arabella Marsh Age 30"* and a stylistic tulip appliqué make up the square for the ninth child of Zachariah and Hannah, born on September 13, 1824. Arabella's husband, *"Walter Marsh Age 32,"* whom she married on September 15, 1852, is depicted with appliquéd oak leaves and acorn reminiscent of her father's block.

Family lore states that the year after Arabella (Aunt Doll) was married, she and Aunt Abby planned and made most of the quilt. The most significant event close to the 1853 date that appears repeatedly on the quilt is the fiftieth Wedding Anniversary of Zachariah and Hannah on September 15, 1852. Again according to family lore, the arrangement of the thirty-six blocks was a problem until "one night Aunt Abby dreamed it out." Filled with excitement, she walked over Green Pond Mountain from her Leach Hollow home in Sherman to her sister Arabella's home on Rocky River. This walk was only a short distance then, but would not be possible today because Candlewood Lake covers it.[3]

This is the only Connecticut family Album quilt documented that is similar to a style frequently attributed to the Quaker style of southeastern Pennsylvania and Delaware. Most of the members of the Zachariah Ferris family were Quaker. The Quaker Hill area of Pawling, New York, was home to other Ferris family members. Pawling shares a boundary with Sherman and is but a few short miles from New Milford. Before the presence of Candlewood Lake, it was an easy journey by foot, by horseback, or by wagon. Here, roads and mountain names echo the names of family members on the route between the two areas. The Ferris family also had strong family ties to Quakers in Delaware.[4]

Zachariah Ferris, age 75, is symbolized as a stately oak tree in the winter of its life. His wife, Hannah, is depicted with a wreath of ivy encircling an anchor and the word *"Hope."*

Three Ferris family members are represented on these two blocks. The flower on the left with the broken stem was made for Edith Leach, who died on March 30, 1832. The pineapple represents her husband, Levi. After Edith's death, Levi married Laura, Edith's sister, who is represented by the flower to his right.

Sampler, 1853, made by Abby Jane Ferris Haviland (1819-1908) and Arabella Ferris March (1824-1887), New Milford, cotton, 93" x 93". Owned by New Milford Historical Society. This quilt tells the story of the Zachariah Ferris family, descendants of one of the founders of New Milford.

Ferris Homestead, c. 1900, in Jerusalem, a section of New Milford now under Candlewood Lake.

Cynthia Wells Standish, Mother and Daughter

"Great elms and oak trees, serene o'er of healing,
Bringing a balm to the hearts which have suffered"[1]

On June 8 and 9,1934, a pageant was presented in Wethersfield to celebrate the tercentennial of the settlement of one of Connecticut's oldest towns. The poem, "The Leaves of the Tree," was woven throughout the pageant and reflected the strength of Wethersfield's affection with its great oaks and elms. These sentinels of nature were honored by the residents of Wethersfield in 1934 just as they had been in 1885 when Cynthia Wells Standish embellished her quilt with their leaves and outlines.

Cynthia Wells was born to Jonathan and Bethankful Andrus Wells on February 26, 1799. A seventh generation descendant of Thomas Wells, Governor of Connecticut in 1655 and 1658, she lived her life in Wethersfield. She married James Standish, a farmer and dairyman on April 2, 1826, and raised seven children, four girls and three boys, born between 1827 and 1842. Both Cynthia and her husband are remembered for their keen interest in political matters, temperance, and religious educational issues.[2] The second child of Cynthia and James Standish, born on July 29, 1829, was also named Cynthia Wells Standish. She remained unmarried and lived her life at the family homestead in Wethersfield.

The Cynthia Wells Standish quilt portrays a family testament to death and the life hereafter. Many things make this two-color quilt outstanding! It is one of the few two-sided quilts documented by the Connecticut Quilt Search Project. Signed and dated *"CWS, 1855,"* it is impossible to determine which Cynthia Wells Standish, the mother, then aged fifty-six, or Cynthia Wells Standish, the daughter, then aged twenty-six, made the quilt.

On one side of the quilt, there are nine oak leaf and reel appliqués. Silhouettes of stately oak trees are planted around the border of the quilt, which is finished with a triple, appliquéd scallop. The reverse of the quilt shows wreaths of elm leaves and elm trees, with their branches shading the peculiar rectangular shapes that face a half-circular white area. This configuration is nearly identical to the placement of the gravestones in the Standish family plot located in "The Ancient Burying Ground of the Wethersfield Village Cemetery."[3]

The gravestone of Cynthia Wells Standish, the mother, is depicted on the quilt. A semi-circular roadway is located similarly in the burial grounds as on the quilt. The grave of Cynthia Wells Standish, the daughter, is in a newer section of the graveyard outside the Ancient Burying Grounds. Cynthia Wells Standish, the mother, died on March 16, 1885, predeceasing her daughter by only three years. Cynthia Wells Standish, the daughter, followed her mother to eternal reward on May 18, 1888 at the age of fifty-nine.

Two-Sided Pictorial, 1855, made by Cynthia Wells Standish, Wethersfield, cotton. Owned by The Wethersfield Historical Society. Both mother and daughter bore the name Cynthia Wells Standish. The configuration at the bottom is that of the family burial site.

The other side of the quilt has Oak Leaf and Reel blocks with an oak tree border.

The gravesites of the Standish family in the Ancient Burying Grounds in Wethersfield.

Sarah Lewis

"Many daughters have done virtuously but thou excellest them all."
—Proverbs 31:29

*I*n the first quarter of the nineteenth century, one woman left her mark on The Second Congregational Church and the residents west of the Mianus River in Greenwich. The name Sarah Lewis was long remembered in the church's history. She never married and was wholly dedicated to the spiritual and social aspects of life, her community, and the world.

Sarah Lewis was born in 1784, the year after the Revolutionary War ended. Her father was Dr. Isaac Lewis, a Yale-educated pastor of The Second Congregational Church for thirty-two years. Lewis Street in Greenwich still commemorates the family.[1] The Lewis household was a sanctuary of spiritual and intellectual inspiration.

"Above all things put on charity which is the bond of perfectness"
—Colossians 3:14

Total gratitude and tribute is paid to Sarah Lewis as the founder and first Superintendent of the Sunday School. She served in this or similar capacities from 1817 and worked to establish the school's library until her death on November 14, 1860. She was a secretary of The Young Ladies Summer Association and her tenure as treasurer for the Stillson Benevolent Society lasted for twenty-five years.[2]

It was said about her, "Always in her place, always judicious in her management, kind and affectionate, self-sacrificing and sincere in all her deportment, she won the confidence and love of the school, and by her teaching and example 'allured to brighter worlds, and led the way'."[3]

"To teach us to number our days that we may apply our hearts unto wisdom"
—Psalms 90:12

The Mariner's Compass quilt was made for Sarah Lewis. The initials of S.A.E. Mead are found on the quilt's back. Also a lifelong member of The Second Congregational Church, Susan A. E. Mead was Sarah's successor as treasurer of the Stillson Benevolent Society. It is thought that the quilt was designed and executed by Susan as the quilt was returned to the family of Susan A. E. Mead after Sarah Lewis's death.

This red, green, and white pieced and appliquéd quilt has nine large compass stars. Each large compass is surrounded by eight intersecting smaller compasses. It is one of the few Connecticut quilts from this time period not made in a block design. The paisley print has been centered on four of the inner triangular points of each compass, large and small. The construction of this quilt was carefully planned and expertly executed. Thrifty use of fabric was not a concern with this quilt. The same green and red fabric borders the quilt with a design resembling interlocking spades.

One hundred and twenty-one names and thirty-five Biblical and inspirational sayings have been scribed on this quilt, including this inscription: *"Presented to Miss Sarah Lewis by the members of the Stillson Benevolent Society, Greenwich, April 15, 1855 'Union is Strength'."* Of the four men's names that appear on this quilt, one is Philander Button, the founder of Greenwich Academy. Also the names of Mr. and Mrs. Joseph Brush, the brother and sister-in-law of Ann Ingersoll Brush, are found on this quilt.

A possible clue about the inspiration for this quilt may be found in "Union is Strength." In approximately 1855, the four Mission Sunday schools in Greenwich, supported by Sarah Lewis's Sunday School at the Second Congregational Church, found it necessary to merge. This was due to the impending Civil War. Two of the mission school superintendents joined the army. The combining of the four schools brought about the establishment of The Union School.[4]

This beautiful quilt was presented to Sarah Lewis five years before her death in November 1860. She served her beloved church through her work in The Stillson Benevolent Society and the Sunday School to her last days. She was convinced that with knowledge and understanding of Biblical verse and the conviction to righteous living her fellow parishioners would be saved. How fitting that the verse she taught and so strongly believed in was then inscribed on her quilt to immortalize her memory for today's worshippers and quilters:

"Something attempted, something done."
—Henry Wadsworth Longfellow

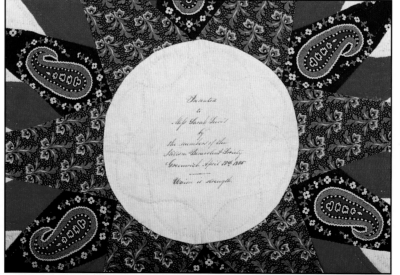

"Presented to Miss Sarah Lewis by the members of the Stillson Benevolent Society, Greenwich, April 15, 1855 'Union is Strength'."

Mariner's Compass. April 15, 1855, made by The Stillson
Benevolent Society, Greenwich, cotton, 99" x 100". Owned by
The Historical Society of the Town of Greenwich.

61

Sarah Jane Barnes's Trousseau Quilts

It was wintertime when Sarah Jane Barnes and Bruce Hodge emerged from the Roxbury Congregational Church on February 9, 1859. The joyful peeling of wedding bells could be heard at their childhood homes a short distance away on South Street. Reverend Austin Isham, their South Street neighbor and the church minister, performed the ceremony, most likely with the entire village in attendance.

Sarah Jane Barnes was born in 1836, the first child of Ashel and Polly Barnes, a farming couple. She spent her childhood in a Greek Revival home at 53 South Street. Robert Bruce Hodge was born on December 25, 1836, to Philo and Lucy Newton Hodge, also of Roxbury. He and his brother were listed as farmers and cattle drovers.

The prosperity of Roxbury was considerable in the 1850s with its all-time high population of 1,114, a number not reached again until the middle of the twentieth century. There were mills, manufactories, shops, and stores, as noted in Helen Hunt W. Humphrey's *Sketches of Roxbury*. Roxbury's main industry, however, was still farming. Sheep were raised for wool, and flax was grown for linen.[1]

In Roxbury today the mills and manufactories are gone and one needs to search hard to find evidence of their existence. Many of the village roads, however, are still dirt and remain unaltered from the mid nineteenth century. On a drive through this quintessential New England village, Colonial capes, Greek Revival, Queen Ann, Federalist, and Georgian Colonial farmhouses abound. The land they occupy is still spacious, open and green. A visit to Roxbury is a visit to the nineteenth century. One can easily imagine the life of Sarah Jane and Bruce when you view their Greek Revival house at 53 South Street.[2]

Sarah and Bruce had three sons, Wallace, Willard, and Burton, but only Willard and Burton lived into adulthood. Sarah died on July 8, 1921 at the age of eighty-four and is buried in the Center Cemetery with her husband and sons.[3] The descendants of Sarah Jane and Bruce and their friends and relatives who signed Sarah Jane's trousseau quilts still walk the roads of Roxbury. They reside in the homes of the settler families of the Booths, Trowbridges, Hurlbutts, Ishams, Kinneys, and Warners.

GOING TO THE SEWING SOCIETY WITH **WILLIMANTIC** THREAD.

THE NATCH LITH. CO. NEW YORK

A Willimantic Thread trade card, c.1880. "Going to the Sewing Society with Willimantic Thread." Sewing Society was another name used for benevolent, circle, or beneficent society. Mostly women attended meetings, however, men were also involved. In Ella Pierce's 1877 Journal from the Litchfield Historical Society, daily entries record carriage rides to the Sewing Society with Sarah Jane Barnes Hodge and her sons, Wallace and Willard.

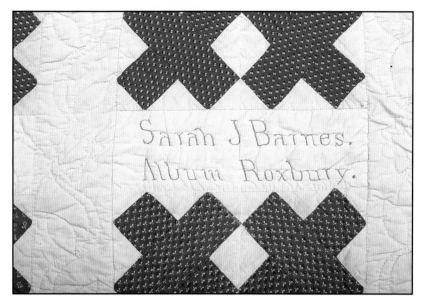

Signed *"Sarah J. Barnes. Album Roxbury."* Quilt researchers may find significance with this inscription. Made c. 1857, Sarah identified her quilt as an "Album."

Octagon Star Album, c. 1852, made by Sarah Jane Barnes Hodge (1836-1921), Roxbury, cotton, 86" x 108". Owned by Philo and Joy Hodge.

Washington Pavement, c. 1857, made by Sarah Jane Barnes Hodge (1836-1921), Roxbury, cotton, 83.5" x 84". Privately owned.

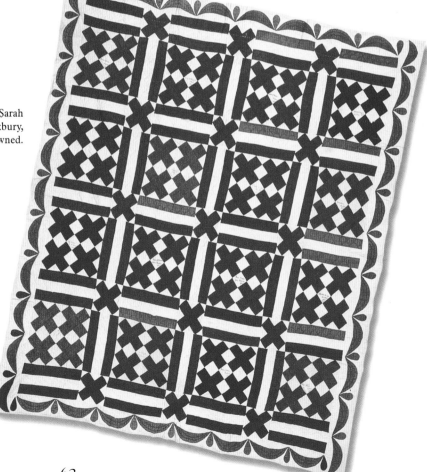

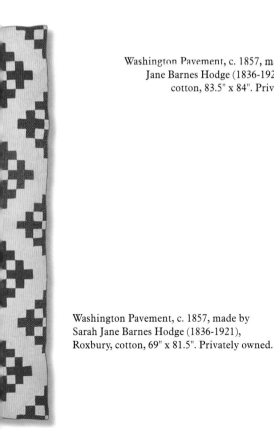

Washington Pavement, c. 1857, made by Sarah Jane Barnes Hodge (1836-1921), Roxbury, cotton, 69" x 81.5". Privately owned.

Sarah Mary Stevens Bailey Russell

Sarah Mary Stevens was born on November 30, 1828 to Gilbert and Marietta Clark Stevens.[1] Both the Stevens and the Clark families were of early Yankee lineage. Sarah was born in the Connecticut River town of Saybrook. Her father worked for the Stevens, Starkey Lumber Company and also served as Deacon in the local Congregational Church. Sarah attended school for a few years and married very young, at the age of fifteen. Martin E. Bailey, Sarah's husband, was eleven years older than she was when they wed in his hometown of Deep River in March of 1844. He was employed as a tinner at the George A. Read & Co. tin manufactory.[2]

Martin and Sarah had one child, a daughter, born June 24, 1850 and named Arianna Pauline. Sarah's excited anticipation of the birth of her child has become part of her family's history. This beautiful red and white quilt was made in celebration of Arianna's birth. It is an exceptionally well-made quilt and has been quilted with ten stitches to the inch.

Around 1854, when Arianna was four years old, Martin Bailey moved his family to Middletown where he began a new occupation as a merchant. On May 9, 1864, when Arianna was only thirteen and Sarah was thirty-five, Martin Bailey died. Young Sarah did not remain a widow. She married Daniel N. Russell of Middletown, who assumed the responsibility of raising teenaged Arianna.

Arianna attended Middletown schools and in the spring of 1870 married Sherman Mitchell Bacon, son of J.P. Bacon. Arianna and Sherman had seven children, although three died before reaching their first birthdays. Sarah was widowed again in 1900. She moved in with her daughter and remained there until her death on October 18, 1905. She is buried in the Fountain Hill Cemetery in Deep River. Her beloved daughter, Arianna, died a few short years later in 1908. Sarah's quilted token of love is the only quilt she ever made and it has passed down through the generations from mother to daughter. The current owner of this lovingly stitched quilt is Sarah's great, great, great granddaughter.

Sarah Mary Stevens Bailey

Wreath of Hearts, c. 1850, made by Sarah Mary Stevens Bailey (1828-1905), Deep River, cotton, 83" x 83". Owned by Rachel E. Schott, daughter of the late Nancy E. Naughton Schott.

Robert Lauder Mathison's Patriotic Civil War Era Quilt

*I*n 1883, Robert Lauder Mathison arrived in Marbledale, Connecticut, as a newlywed with his wife, Catherine Robert Hartland, whom he married on June 11, 1882. He served as the minister at St. Andrew's Episcopal Church on the Litchfield Turnpike in Marbledale from 1883 to 1885. This tiny village in the Litchfield Hills, set along the banks of the Aspetuck River, was once a nineteenth-century industrial center with twenty-one stone sawmills. Approximately thirty thousand feet of marble was cut and sold annually out of Marbledale, Connecticut, before Vermont Marble became popular.[1]

Born in Guilford on June 20, 1839, Reverend Mathison was the fifth Robert Lauder Mathison. The original Mathisons came from Scotland. His grandfather, Robert Lauder Mathison, fought in the American Revolution. Reverend Mathison attended Wesleyan College in New York, receiving his degree in 1860, and his descendants still have his sheepskin diploma. He received his local preacher certificate from the Methodist Episcopal Church in 1872; however, he was not ordained as an Episcopal minister until 1876.[2] Catherine and Robert had one son, Edward Thompson Mathison, who also became an Episcopalian minister serving at St. Andrew's. His granddaughter, Flora Mathison Cummings, born in 1899, remembers watching her grandfather piece quilts by a window in the twilight, sewing by the last rays of sunlight, before his death on December 31, 1919. Flora lived to be ninety-nine and just died in 1998.

Written on the hexagon mosaic quilt is, *"Brooklyn N. Y. E. Conf. 1861."* There are also ninety-six names of men scribed on this quilt, including two by the name of Ino W. Roberts and Francis Burns, Africa. R.L. Mathison is one of the names listed. Unfortunately, the purpose for the Conference remains unknown. The archives of the Episcopal Church have records of youth conferences back to 1869 only. It may very well be that this is the only record of the event that occurred in Brooklyn, New York, known as the "N.Y.E. Conference of 1861." The onset of the Civil War could explain the patriotic use of red, white, and blue colors for the quilt.

Robert Lauder Mathison

Stained glass window dedicated to the quiltmaker, St. Andrew's Episcopal Church, Marbledale.

Hexagon Mosaic, c. 1861, made by Robert Lauder Mathison, Westbrook, cotton, 70" x 98.5". Owned by Marcy Fuller Gustafson.

Mary Esther Hoyt Smith

Hardship came to Mary Esther Hoyt early in her life. At the age of eight, her father, Josiah, a dealer of leather, died leaving his wife, Mary "Polly" Warren Hoyt, and their eleven children. Mary Esther was the sixth child, born on September 14, 1807. Her family had relative prosperity until the British embargoes began in 1807 and the fear of British attack that came with the War of 1812. Mary Esther would have been old enough to remember the British patrol boats and the subsequent rallying of local forces to protect their Connecticut lands and harbors.

Mary Esther married George Edwin Smith on January 21, 1827 at the age of twenty. George came from a large and respectable Norwalk family. Together they raised a family of six children in South Norwalk, an area then known as "Old Well."[1] It was through Mary Esther's only daughter that her prized quilt was passed down. Family lore records that the quilt was made when Mary Esther was in her fifties.

Mary Esther lived out her last years of life with her daughter, Jane Smith Albertson. Her quilt has been passed down through five generations of family women who have cherished this beautiful textile heirloom.

Sunflower, c. 1840-1865, made by Mary Esther Hoyt Smith (1807-1898), South Norwalk, cotton, 81" x 90.5". Owned by Charlotte Craig, daughter of Carolyn Craig.

Woodcut from *History and Antiquities* by John Warner Barber, 1836.

Eastern view of the village of Old Well, Norwalk.

Mary Esther Hoyt Smith

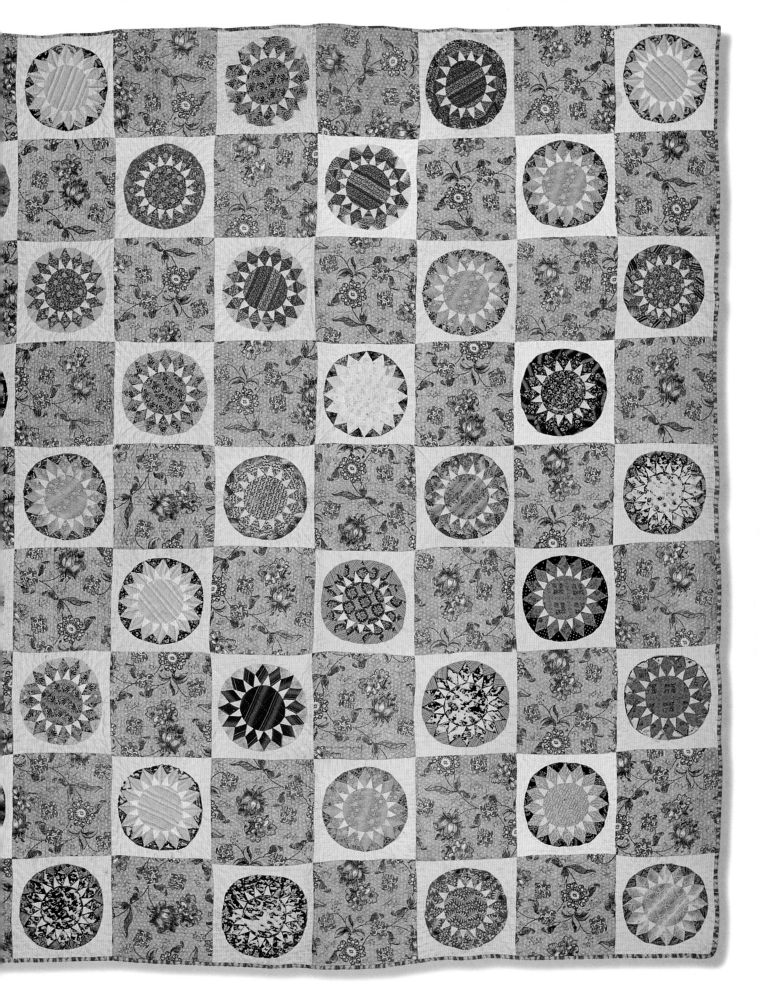

Sisters! Let us gird ourselves anew![1]

Familiarity between men and women was rarely addressed or made reference to in Puritan society, especially during addresses by invited preachers; however, the 1865 afternoon address by Rev. S.B.S. Bissell disregarded that taboo. Bissell's sermon was in celebration of the 150th anniversary of the Second Congregational Church of Greenwich, Connecticut. His special attention was directed to The Stillson Benevolent Society, with this statement: "Now let me fall into the hands of the ladies, not into the hands of the gentlemen of the Second Congregational Church of Greenwich."[2]

His praise was bestowed upon one of the most active and successful churchwomen's group in the state in 1865. The Female Charitable Society of Greenwich originated on November 17, 1811. In an account kept by Sarah Lewis, its treasurer, there are many references to large amounts of cloth, quilts, and battings. In 1821, Elizabeth Stillson was the first secretary of the Young Ladies Summer Association of the Second Congregational Church of Greenwich. The first season's meetings included inspirational readings, collection of $20 in donations, $7.50 in subscriptions, and $58.75 in articles, an occasional address by Rev. Dr. Lewis, the sewing of eleven garments, two bed-quilts, one cradle quilt, three pairs of pillow cases, packing "the box" for the missions, and concluding with song and prayer.

In 1829, the Young Ladies Summer Association was renamed the Stillson Benevolent Society in memory of Elizabeth Stillson. Members worked tirelessly during more than thirty meetings a year earning monies and packing boxes to be sent first to missions abroad and then to the West. In 1833, they produced twelve bed quilts and held a private sale that spawned annual fairs. Quilts made at their meetings were the highlights of these sales. Frequently, they were sold for the exorbitant amounts of $20 to $30.

In 1862, The Stillson Benevolent Society made this beautiful signature quilt. The red print and white appliqué quilt is signed *Made for Miss Sarah Mead by the ladies of the Stillson Benevolent Society, Greenwich, May 13, 1862.* The pattern is most unusual. The Connecticut Quilt Search Project chose to call it Oak Leaf variation. Barbara Brackman's *Encyclopedia of Appliqué* book documents a very close pattern found in Ruth Finley's *Old Patchwork Quilts and the Women Who Made Them* identifying this as "Tobacco Leaf." Brackman's *Encyclopedia of Appliqué* also shows a pattern called Lobster, which closely resembles this one. We know that Connecticut is the Charter Oak State and we also know that tobacco was one of its biggest crops. This quilt was made in the shoreline town of Greenwich, also a port, so the Lobster pattern could be considered. Once again, similar to many other nineteenth-century Connecticut quilts, there is a swag border setting off this cotton quilt.[3]

The Stillson Benevolent Society was founded in 1811 and was one of the earliest charitable societies in Connecticut.

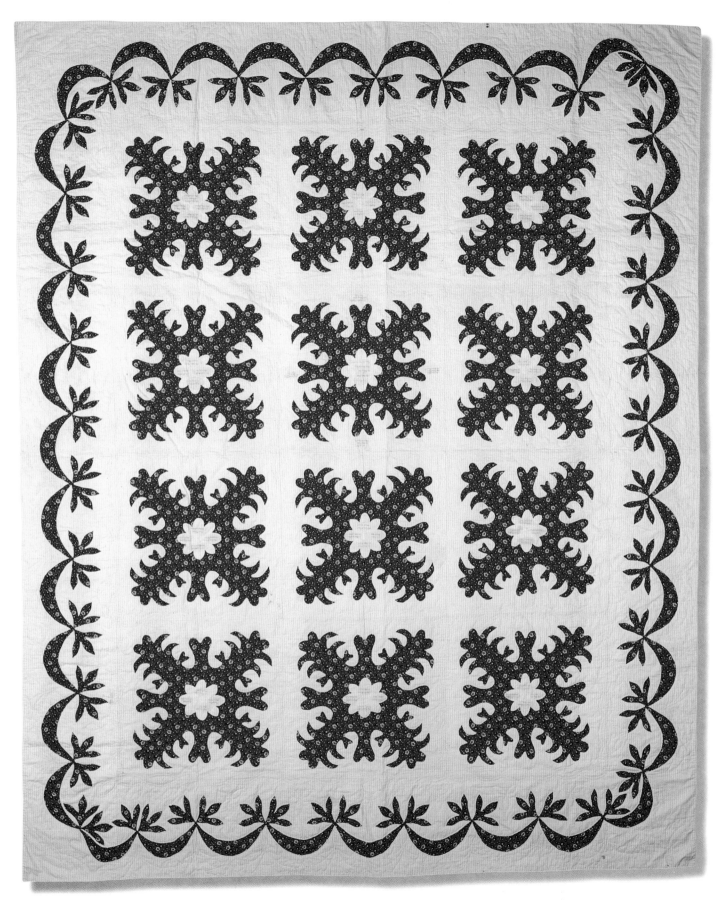

Oak Leaf Variation, 1862, made by The Stillson Benevolent Society,
Greenwich, cotton, 83" x 101". Owned by The Historical Society of
the Town of Greenwich.

Medallion Baby Quilt

*H*arriet Beecher Stowe in her book, *The Minister's Wooing*, surely had this type of quilt in mind when she wrote:

> The good wives of New England, impressed with that thrifty orthodoxy of economy which forbids to waste the merest trifle, had a habit of saving every scrap clipped out in the fashioning of household garments, and these they cut into fanciful patterns and constructed of them rainbow shapes and quaint traceries, the arrangement of which became one of their few fine art.[1]

At first sight, this forty inch by forty inch baby quilt is reminiscent of the famous Connecticut Copp family quilt from Stonington, which is now in The Smithsonian Institute. Grace Rogers Cooper's descriptive verse, *"The greatest treasure trove, however, is the variety of printed dress fabrics"* could also be applied to this quilt, documented in Manchester.[2] It has hundreds of scraps of fabric in a framed design, which required much patience in the piecing. Most impressive is the tiny size of the four patches on point in a square that *could* bring disarray to the quilt's center: instead it brings a softened, wandering amazement to the eye. In mint condition, it is hard to believe that this quilt covered its intended infant for long.

There are actually five borders to this quilt ending, with the nine patch squares. Not satisfied with a plain backing, or in an effort to use up all of her scraps, the maker created the back of the quilt as a strip quilt of triangles and sawtooth triangles, thus fabricating a remarkable two-sided quilt.

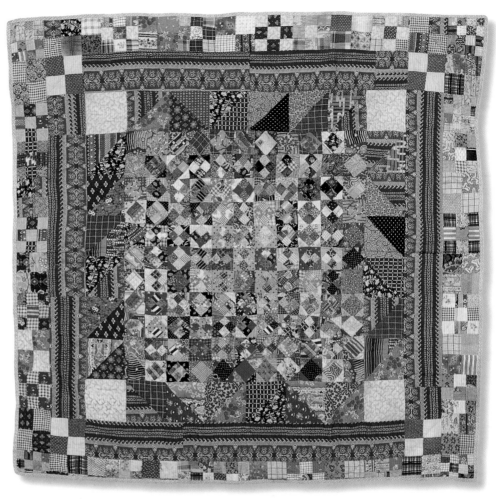

Medallion Scrap Quilt, c. 1840-1865, made by a Manning-Greene family member, Manchester, cotton, 40" x 40". Owned by Dr. Pierre and Judith Gates Marteney.

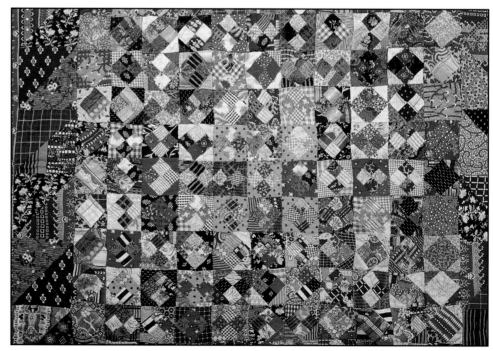

The center of the quilt contains pieces measuring less than an inch.

A thrifty quiltmaker used her scraps for both sides of this two-sided quilt.

Mary Jane Cole Dickenson

Mary Jane Cole was born in 1841 to Eliza Brown (1801-1877) and Abner Cole (1797-1860) of Middlefield. Eliza received a handmade chest as part of her wedding outfit, possibly from her father, upon her marriage to Abner. She passed the chest along with its contents of locks of children's hair, family bibles, and albums to her oldest daughter, Mary Jane, when Mary Jane married Linus Dickenson of Wethersfield in 1864.

Family members believe that it was Mary who made the quilt; she was renown for her quilting skills. Linus and Mary had five children, among them Edwin Cole Dickenson (1880-1956) who served as a judge on the Connecticut Supreme Court.

Mary passed the quilt and chest on to her oldest daughter, Gertrude Evangeline Dickenson (1868-1967), who married Arthur Shew of Wethersfield in 1899. A copy of the newspaper account of their wedding, as well as her wedding dress, were found in the chest. The account includes mention of the fact that "the presents were numerous and costly" and that the bride was "becomingly attired in white silk." Prior to her marriage, Gertrude was the first woman ever to graduate from Hartford Public High School, the second oldest school in the country. She then became a teacher where, according to the same newspaper article, she was "held in high esteem by a large circle of friends."

Arthur and Gertrude had three children and she in turn passed the chest and quilt to her only daughter, Helen Evangeline Shew (1906-1979), when Evangeline married Harrison David Schofield of Hartford in 1929. Harrison and Helen had two children and Helen passed the family heirloom onto her only daughter, Susan Shew Schofield (1932-2001), when Susan married George C. Duggan of Hartford in 1958. George and Susan had three children and she passed the quilt and chest to her youngest daughter, the present owner.

Today, Mary's descendants continue to do as their ancestors did, adding personal treasures to the chest, and inscribing their names on the lid, thereby further enriching a wonderful heritage of lives and loves for the next generation.

©Amy Duggan

Stars Upon Stars Variation, c. 1840-1865, made by Mary J. Cole Dickenson, Wethersfield, cotton, 81" x 98". Owned by Amy J. Duggan.

Mary J. Cole Dickenson

This chest contains photographs of the four generations of women who have owned the quilt. Clockwise, from top left: Mary J. Cole Dickenson, Gertrude E. Dickenson Shew, Susan S. Schofield Duggan, and Helen E. Shew Schofield.

Mary's descendants continue to inscribe their names on the inside lid of the trunk that has been passed from mother to daughter upon the daughter's marriage.

Post Civil War Sampler

Ladies Benevolent Society of the Second Baptist Church of New London

Tarrytown Sanitary Commission

"A few 'tired Soldiers' in the Cause met at the Parsonage…"[1]

The Ladies Benevolent Society of the Second Baptist Church of New London left their Sampler quilt and from the Ladies Benevolent Society of Northfield remain the minutes of their activities from 1842 to 1886. Each artifact becomes an historic testament to endless charitable deeds. Sadly, the New London Benevolent Society is no longer in existence and the quilts recorded in the log of the Northfield ladies have not been found. Both groups, however, were comprised of women doing their part for the soldiers of the Civil War.

On December 25, 1861, the Ladies Benevolent Society of Northfield changed its name to the Northfield Soldier's Aid Association. As was written in their minutes in 1863, "with *determined hearts* to do all in their power for the aid of 'Our Brave Soldiers…'"[2] The stress and exhaustion of their work during this dark period of America's history was recorded on November 3, 1863 with "a few 'tired Soldiers' in the Cause met at the Parsonage…"[3] Weary from the hardships of war and consumed in supporting the military companies from their towns, they continued to press on in their effort. They regularly packed barrels of necessary items required for the medical care of the troops or to supplement their provisions in the field.

The U.S. Sanitary Commission was one of the receiving organizations. The Commission was charged with providing and distributing medical supplies to the sick and wounded men of the Civil War and to relieve the anxiety of relatives on the home front. Not only did they provide funds, clothing, blankets, food, bandages, and other emergency items, they also strove to provide a better understanding of battle-incurred injury and disease to prevent further disintegration of the human condition.[4] Women's organizations such as the benevolent societies, beneficent societies, Sunday schools, sewing societies, and missionary societies were generally affiliated with the church. These groups made these massive contributions of supplies and provided the framework of the U.S. Sanitary Commission.

In 1867, the New London ladies donated sampler blocks and constructed a quilt most likely to raise funds for war veterans. Symbols of patriotism, agriculture, a seafaring community, and the remembrance of death decorate the quilt. All of the blocks are pieced and/or appliquéd with the exception of an embroidered hen near the quilt's center. The quilt has been passed down for over 130 years through the family of Louisa Cottrell Winslow.

The records of the Ladies Benevolent Society of the tiny village of Northfield span forty-four years of biweekly meetings and activities. Their name was changed five times to reflect the focus of their good deeds and the events of the time. The meetings always commenced with prayer and spiritual readings or a presentation about social issues such as temperance. The weekly activities included quilting or the production of clothing and bed linens. Boxes of textiles and food goods were regularly packed and sent to Home Missions in Ohio and the Home for the Friendless. Quilts were worked on for members of their society or people in the village. Men also attended these gatherings, and are listed as dues-paying members. Their donations were double that charged for women. It was the duty of the men to provide the spiritual readings and discourse.

When the Civil War ended members continued to work for the veterans and added the "Home for the Friendless"[5] to their enterprises. In 1865, a quilt they finished in September was "carried to the Agricultural Fair and received a Premium of $1.00."[6] In 1866, they held a Festival that included a quilt show. The festival was the beginning of fundraising for their new church. During the harvest time, their meetings were suspended for a short time, as they recorded "Meetings deferred through Haying."[7]

By 1879, meetings of the Association were no longer held. By 1881, however, the ladies were back together for a new cause. This time it was for the benefit of their church and themselves. They held fundraising dinners to build and furnish the kitchen in the church basement. They now called themselves "The Ladies Improvement Society."[8] Their activities that year involved sewing and knitting to raise funds for the "Home for the Friendless"[9] and also to purchase a carpet for the new church. Their zeal for working in a group for benevolent purposes was ended by 1885-86. The number of ladies in the "Old Sewing Society,"[10] as it was now renamed, was greatly reduced. Now, instead of working on quilts, they tacked and bound "comfortables" or tied comforters.

The existence of these women's organizations can be found in nearly every history of Connecticut's towns and villages. The earliest began in the Congregational churches in the beginning of the nineteenth century. A Female Foreign Missionary Society was formed in Greenwich at the Second Congregational Church around 1815.[11] Membership for women in benevolent societies, anti-slavery groups, and temperance societies was encouraged; however, they were sometimes prevented from taking an active role in the latter two groups. In 1828, a Temperance Society including men and women was formed in Canterbury and Plainfield. The names of Prudence Crandall, founder of Canterbury's Miss Crandall's Boarding School for "young ladies and misses of color," and her sister-in-law, Clarissa Crandall, are recorded as members.[12] Despite female membership, the rules of the meeting prohibited any woman to speak in public. If she desired to communicate at all, it had to be passed to the chairman to be read by a male.[13]

In South Woodstock, the Female Charitable Cent Society was formed in 1816. The fee for membership for the year was fifty-two cents or one penny/a week. Members worked to give funds to the "Heathen Cherokee Children and other Heathen Children."[14]

"Quiltins" that once provided warmth and comfort for their families had expanded into female charitable societies, sewing circles, and missionary societies: "Women continued to sew, quilt or embroider but they shaped their meetings into quite different occasions to meet together."[15] These women influenced the heart and soul of our country not from the pulpit, platform, or stage, but through their home industry and benevolent work for the benefit of all.

Sampler, 1864, made by members of the Sanitary Commission of Tarrytown, New York, Tarrytown, New York, cotton, 76" x 95". Owned by Mr. and Mrs. Charles E. Crocker, Jr.

Sampler, 1867, made by the Ladies Benevolent Society of the Second Baptist Church of New London, New London, cotton, 77" x 89". Owned by Bob and Patty Norman.

Scrap Quilt, c. 1868, made by Egbert Newberry, Newington, cotton, 32" x 33". Privately owned. As a young boy, Egbert had to help his mother with the wash each Monday morning and in the afternoon he had to learn how to sew, which he considered "a girl's job." During the Civil War, he suffered a severe spinal injury after his horse was shot out from under him and thereafter he walked with crutches and could not even dress himself without help. His much-dreaded sewing lessons were to prove useful, however, as he augmented the family income by piecing quilts for pay, and by doing the family mending. This charming quilt was made in commemoration of the birth of his granddaughter, Mary Newberry Storrs, on December 19, 1868.

Egbert Newberry

Anna Hasson Melvin

Anna Hasson Melvin

*T*his delightful One-Patch quilt beams with the personality and tenacity of the maker. Anna Hasson was born on October 31, 1835 in St. Anicett, Canada, one of eight children of Elizabeth Lockhart Hasson and William James Hasson. Her father emigrated from an area near Glasgow, Scotland, so perhaps it was his trip that provided the wanderlust that inspired Anna to move to Massachusetts when she was eighteen years old to live with a brother who had moved there before her. On May 10, 1860, she married George Melvin, an immigrant from Tullamore, King's Count, Ireland.

Their new life together led them to the rural farmland of Salisbury, in the northwest corner of Connecticut. They settled into a place they would call home for the rest of their lives. Anna and her husband adapted well to farm life and raised three sons and a daughter in the pastoral surroundings. Besides being remembered as a wonderful cook, Anna made a number of quilts, most likely for utilitarian purposes given their rural lifestyle. It is one small mention in their family history that also connects Anna to quilting. Handed down with her quilts was the record that, although Anna enjoyed excellent health, she became blind for the last four years of her life—and blamed it all on the quilting!

Scrap Quilt, c. 1840-1865, made by Anna Hasson Melvin (1835-1921), Salisbury, cotton, 78" x 83". Owned by Eleanor Sheldon Kern.

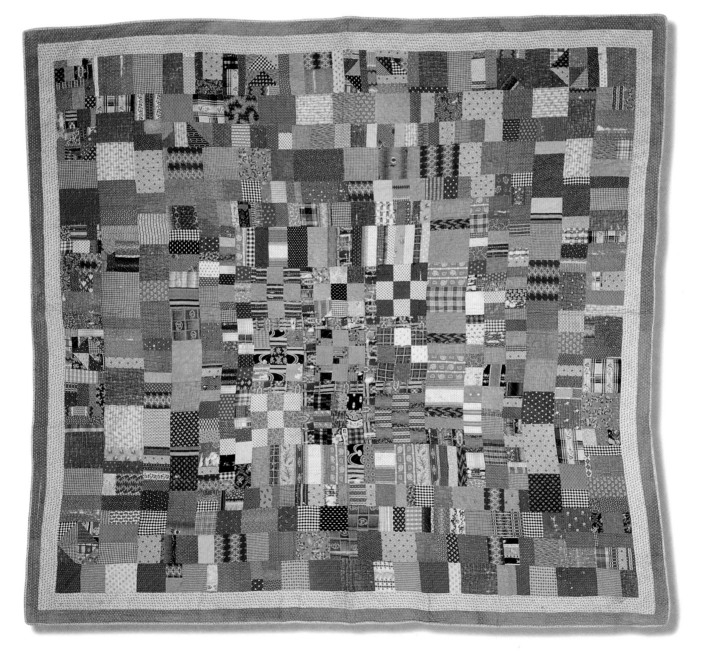

Lois Hotchkiss

"The General Run of People."[1]

This spinning wheel, which passed through the generations of the Hotchkiss family, was used to spin the flax woven for the backing of Lois Hotchkiss' One-Patch quilt. Lois was born in Waterbury to Tamar Richardson and Stephen Hotchkiss on November 28, 1795. Lois was the fifth of their seven children. Her father was in Capt. Phineas Porter's camp in Waterbury. He was a member of the First Church and a deacon from 1809-1826.[2]

The Hotchkiss family's homestead was located on East Mountain near the western side of the Naugatuck River. Although Lois never married, she helped parent the twelve nieces and nephews of her sister, Esther. Her family was plagued with the early deaths of a sister, a brother, and a brother-in-law. When Stephen, her father and the family patriarch, died on September 9, 1826, the family was left to live on Stephen's soldier's pension. At the time, there were few wealthy people in Waterbury; they were considered the "general run" of people. The widow Tamar Hotchkiss owned and operated the family's cider mill and this family operation supplied their neighbors with the standard table liquid of the time.[3]

As a young lady, Lois would have visited her friends with her spinning wheel in tow. It was said that "the little wheel was a familiar friend and women (of Waterbury) had the sensible habit of finding pleasure in work."[4] Many families hired itinerant weavers. In 1818, John Morse was a noted weaver in Waterbury who exchanged his weaving services for board and his expenses. His cloth would go to making stockings, pantaloons, silk vests, shirting, woolen, linen and cotton cloth. His fee for two and a half yards of linen cloth was $1.00, two yards of woolen cost $2.66, and four yards of cotton was $1.75.[5]

Few people had carriages in Waterbury, so the entire Hotchkiss family traveled to church by horseback. A large piece of cloth was attached to the saddle with the extra rider backwards facing the horse's tail. This method was known as "ride and tie."[6] Because of Stephen's position as a deacon in the First Church, it was important that his family be an exemplar model for others. In the winter, they endured an unheated meetinghouse, managing minimal warmth from their foot-stoves. In the summer, turkey feather fans were used to circulate air and the somnolent congregation chewed on a concoction of fennel, caraway, and dill called "meetin seed."[7]

Lois' mother died on March 29, 1853 at age ninety-four.[8] In 1896, she was remembered as one of only fourteen in the Old Burying Ground to live beyond the age of ninety. Her daughter's quilt, the single block on point with sashing, is simple but elegant. Lois linked the quilt to her mother's generation with the backing of the quilt, a plain white cloth initialed *"TR"* for her mother, Tamar, providing their ancestors with this cherished heirloom.

Spinning wheel used to spin the flax which was used to weave the linen for the backing.

Backing showing hand-woven linen and initials *"TR."*

One-Patch, c. 1865-1890, made by Lois Hotchkiss (1795-1884), Waterbury, cotton, 78" x 94". Privately owned. Lois' mother, Tamar Richardson Hotchkiss, spun and wove the backing before she was married.

Humphreysville Album Quilt

*I*n the early 1800s most Connecticut farmers still practiced conservative agricultural techniques. Because of competition from fertile western lands, many agricultural leaders demanded that inefficient colonial farming practices be reformed. This would increase farm productivity and at the same time help stem emigration from the State. Ellsworth Grant in his book, *Yankees Dreamers and Doers*, noted that General David Humphreys "urged Connecticut farmers to stop emigration by enriching their land through hard work, the spreading of manure, and rotating their crops…only perseverance in agricultural improvements could restore commerce and industry."[1]

One of the leaders of agricultural reform was General David Humphreys, appointed by President John Adams to serve as Minister to Spain. During the time Humphreys served in Spain, he familiarized himself with the production and use of wool from Merino sheep. Humphreys was recalled from his diplomatic post in 1802 when Thomas Jefferson became President. The Spanish government allowed him to ship a flock of one hundred Merino sheep—seventy-five ewes and twenty-five rams—to his farm in Derby. Francis Little in her book, *Early American Textiles*, noted "one thing the American manufacturer lacked was good wool. The finest quality came from Spain where cross-breeding had been carried on scientifically for generations."[2]

The Embargo of 1807 prevented the importation of foreign wool. The demand for local wool increased, but it was of poor quality. When Napoleon invaded Spain in 1807 he seized thousands of Merino sheep and sent them to Britain and France; from there, many found their way into this country. The excellent quality of wool now available resulted in the increase of woolen factories, and the demand for Merino sheep breeding increased the production of wool as well.[3] The wool obtained from those sheep was of excellent quality and sold for $2.50 per pound. Because of the demand for these sheep, the animals sold for as much as $2,000 for the rams and $1,000 for the ewes.

In 1803, David Humphreys had built a woolen mill at Humphreysville, now Seymour, for the manufacturing of broadcloth that sold for $4.50 a yard. This mill ran by waterpower.[4] The twenty-foot cascade at Rimmon Falls was already being used by a scythe works, two fulling mills, and a sawmill. Humphrey purchased all the mills and privileges for $2,647 in 1803.[5] He learned the operation of a mill in England, purchased improved machinery, and then started his operation. Because of the labor shortage that existed and also to obtain cheap labor, New York orphans from almshouses and young women fresh off the farms were brought in to work the mill. Orphans could be hired as cheap labor, female workers were paid much less than men, and children were paid much less than the women. Boarding houses were built to house the orphans and young women.

At his inauguration in 1809, President Madison wore a suit of clothes made from cloth manufactured at this mill.[6] The reputation of the mill for producing quality cloth was the finest in the country. Jefferson, upon hearing of the excellent quality of the cloth, also ordered suiting from this mill. By 1811, Humphreys' New England village became the first model factory village consisting of three churches, fifty-six dwellings, and three mercantile stores.[7] A school was also established, with Humphreys paying the salary of the schoolmaster. He instituted moral codes and all workers were expected to conform to these codes or risk being discharged. As time progressed, other manufacturers entered the textile field and created mills that were to surpass the village of Humphreysville. When the War of 1812 ended, the country was again flooded with foreign imports selling well below the price that could be manufactured for profit in this country. As a consequence, many mills struggled to survive. To protect domestic manufacturing, Congress in 1816 passed the first protective tariff on woolen goods.[8] In 1822, Walm and Leaming, a commission house located in Philadelphia, purchased one half of the Humphreysville factory.[9] Shortly, thereafter, the factory ceased operation. In 1899, Humphreys was honored as "The Founder of the New England Factory Village," according to the National Association of Wool Manufacturers.[10]

S. E. view of Humphreysville, in Derby.

Woodcut from *History and Antiquities* by John Warner Barber, 1836.

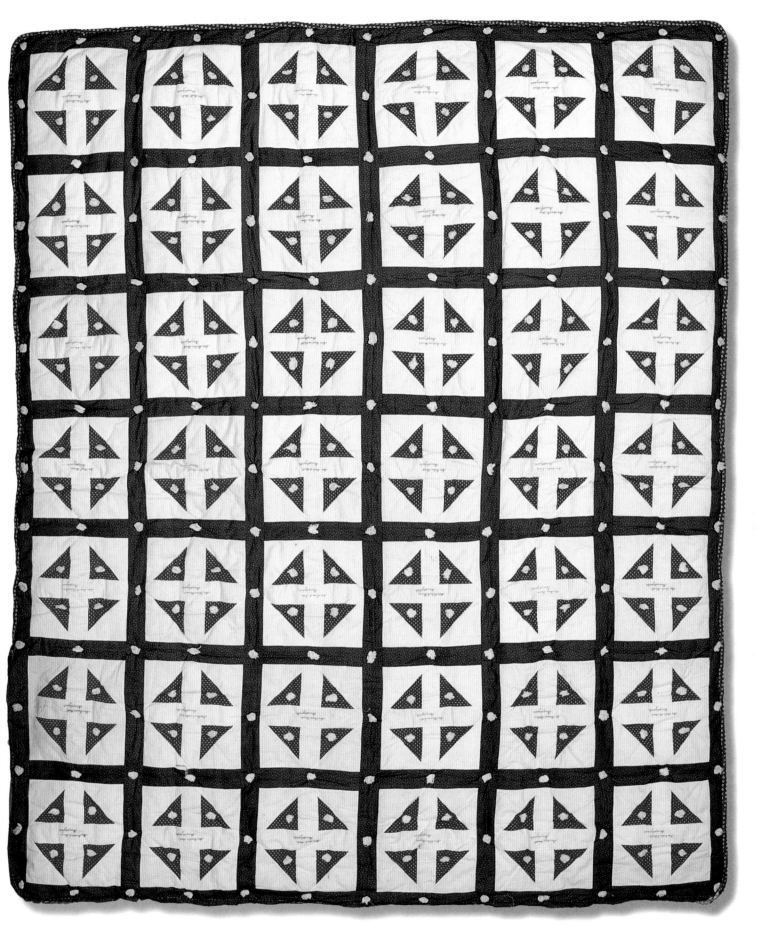

Humphreysville Album Quilt, c. 1840–1865, made by members of the Beecher Family, Humphreysville, cotton, 73.5" x 83.5". Owned by The Seymour Historical Society. Each block contains a hand written name and the words *"Humphreysville, Connecticut."* The handwriting appears to be the same. It was not unusual in those days for one person with elegant handwriting skills to pen all the information on a quilt.

Mary A. Beers

The year was 1910, in Cincinnati, Ohio: Goodin, Reid & Co., the makers of Reddisole cotton batt, sponsored the Reddisole Revolutionary Quilt Contest. Entrance required that the quiltmaker be connected with one of the descendants of the "Sons of Battle" in the American Revolution. This national competition was first managed through local dry goods store carrying Goodin, Reid & Co. batts. The Howlands Dry Goods store of Bridgeport sponsored Connecticut's state competition.

Mrs. Otis B. Curtiss had inherited a Mariner's Compass quilt made by her great aunt, Mary A. Beers. Mary's father, Silas, served in the Revolutionary War as a drummer of the 5th Connecticut Regiment, beating the march to the battlefront at Ticonderoga. His service was also enlisted for the War of 1812, forty years later. Having Revolutionary War ties, Mary Beer's heirloom quilt qualified and was entered in the quilt competition along with 103 other entries.

First place went to Mrs. F.E. Price for her quilt with a design called Washington Army. Second place was granted to Mrs. Hurlbutt for her appliqué quilt with a "pattern so padded with cotton that the flowers and leaves are raised."[1] Third place was claimed by the Mariner's Compass quilt. Other quilt patterns displayed were recorded as Washington's Plume, Rising Sun, Old Maid's Patience, and Bow-Knot. As one of the top three winners, Mary Beers' quilt became eligible to travel to Cincinnati for the National Competition.

Mrs. Otis Curtiss received an early Christmas present that year. On December 21, 1910, a congratulatory letter arrived from the Goodin, Reid & Co. with a first prize check for $100. On return to Connecticut, her quilt was displayed with great pride at the Stratford Congregational Church along with eighty other bed quilts from the area. A Bridgeport newspaper described it as "A miracle of fine needlework."

Mariner's Compass, c. 1840-1865, made by Mary A. Beers, Bridgeport, cotton and linen, 92.5" x 95.5". Owned by Stratford Historical Society.

Henrietta Smith Glover – Mother-in-Law

*H*enrietta Smith was the second born child of Sally and Henry A. Smith from Danish Farms, a section of Derby in Fairfield County. As one of the oldest girls in a farming family of eight, learning sewing skills must have been a necessity of life for Henrietta. Family documentation records that she made her Queen Victoria's Crown quilt with the help of her mother and her sisters: Elorsa Louisa, Adeline Augusta, and Sarah Ann Smith. This most unusual quilt contains a myriad of triangles pointed in all directions. The quilt's flying geese diagonal sashings end and blend into borders of the geese in flight pattern. The quilt was made between 1840 and 1865.

Henrietta was married to Henry Glover, of Newtown, on March 20, 1838. At the beginning of their marriage, Henry was studying to be a parson in the Universalist church. "On account of a weakness in his voice, which broke down under the effort to preach," he had to give up his ministerial aspirations.[1] Over the next twenty years, he pursued teaching in Westport, the stove business in Bridgeport, farming in Brookfield, and finally settled his family in Huntington in the dairy farming and gardening business. They had two sons, Theophilus, who was a minister in Brooklyn, and Henry Fordyce Glover, who was born on December 2, 1842. Henry lived his life with his parents managing the family homestead.[2]

At the turn of the century, Henrietta was in failing health. The family enlisted help from a young neighbor, Elma O. Bolles. She was the daughter of Henry and Sarah E. Reeves Bolles. Around 1899, at the age of sixteen, Elma went to live at the Glover homestead to assist in Henrietta's care. Henrietta died about a year later, and Elma stayed on as housekeeper for Henrietta's son, Henry Fordyce. The propriety of the day, however, did not allow unmarried ladies of any age to live with a man. So on November 28, 1906, at the age of sixty-four, Henry Fordyce proposed to and married Elma O. Bolles, age twenty-three. Perhaps because of their age difference, Elma always referred to her husband as "Mr. Glover." Their short union produced no children and Henry Fordyce died on October 8, 1912, only six years after his marriage to Elma.

The Star with Baskets quilt and the Carolina Lily were also made by Henrietta Glover. The Carolina Lily set on point is simple in comparison to the medallion Star with Baskets with its fifteen borders. Besides the fabrics, there are other subtle similarities in the quilts. The Carolina Lily pattern reappears in the medallion quilt; this time set straight as one of the borders but with triangles in baskets. Both quilts have thin batting to allow ease in achieving the eight to nine quilting stitches per inch in a clam shell pattern.

The young widow Elma married Edwin Bassett in 1917. Within two years, she found herself once again a widow and once again remarried, this time to Samuel Harper of England. It was through their son Ralph Bolles Harper that the quilts were passed down to the present owner. The quilts frequently cover a handsome Empire bed at the Glover Homestead in Huntington.

Henrietta Smith Glover

Elma Olive Bolles

The quiltmaker demonstrated her skill and creativity in piecing her basket borders.

Star with Baskets, c. 1865-1890, made by Henrietta Smith Glover (1818-1900), Huntington, cotton, 84" x 89". Owned by John Bolles, III.

Queen Victoria's Crown, c. 1840-1865, made by Henrietta Smith Glover (1818-1900), Huntington, cotton, 84" x 89". Owned by John Bolles, III.

Carolina Lily, c. 1865-1890, made by Henrietta Smith Glover (1818-1900), Huntington, cotton, 84" x 89". Owned by John Bolles, III.

Mary Ann Hoadley Seymour Tomlinson

The one hundred and twelve names on this Mosaic pattern cotton quilt are the friends and family members of Mary Ann Hoadley Seymour Tomlinson. As the privileged daughter of Silas Hoadley, Mary Ann grew up during the heyday of Plymouth's clock-manufacturing years. Her father came from Bethany and was a carpenter until about ten years before Mary Ann's birth. Around 1809, he associated himself with Eli Terry and Seth Thomas in the manufacturing of the wooden clocks Connecticut is noted for. The manufacturing village set up for production was called Hoadleyville. Their partnership continued for only four years before both Mr. Terry and Mr. Thomas began their own clock business ventures. Silas Hoadley continued making clocks in Plymouth until 1849.[1]

Mary Ann was the last of four children born to Silas and Sarah Painter Hoadley on May 4, 1814. At the age of twenty-two, she married George B. Seymour of Washington on September 2, 1836. George died shortly after and Mary Ann married George Tomlinson of Plymouth on June 17, 1840. She and George Tomlinson had three children.[2] The mosaic block on the quilt inscribed with *"Mary Ann Tomlinson – MOTHER"* indicates that this signature quilt was made for one of their four children, Milo, Amy, Robert or Ammi, around 1870. Family relatives named Seymour, Mitchell, Tomlinson, and Hoadley are inscribed in addition to many other family names. The quilt was passed down from one of Mary Ann's children to granddaughter Eunice Tomlinson Allen and then to great-granddaughter Clarabel Allen Froeliger.

East view of the central part of Plymouth.

Woodcut from *History and Antiquities* by John Warner Barber, 1836.

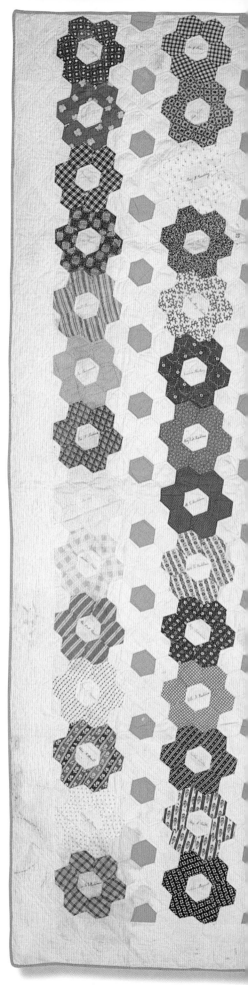

Mosaic, c. 1870, made by Mary Ann Hoadley Seymour Tomlinson (1819-1893), Plymouth, cotton, 82" x 82". Owned by Plymouth Historical Society.

89

Nellie L. Gates Ransbotham

The town of Hartland, settled in 1754, is situated in the north central part of Connecticut and borders Massachusetts. The terrain of Hartland was created by the flow of ice creating a valley with mountains to the east and west with a stream running through it, later to be known as the East branch of the Farmington River. This division of land is referred to by the residents as West Hartland, Hartland Hollow, and East Hartland; however, all are in the town of Hartland. Hartland Hollow no longer exists. In 1940, the people were moved upland, the cemetery was relocated, and the area was flooded to create the present Barkhamsted Reservoir.

In the period between 1791 and 1817, saw-mills and grist-mills began to flourish in the area. It was not unusual to see as many as ten mills in a small village. It was crucial to locate the mill beside a waterway since the only power used at that time was waterpower. Many mills were located in the West Hartland area and it was in this area that John Ward opened a business to manufacture calico. Local ponds provided the necessary water and mill owners purchased rights from landowners to build dams. Power for Ward's Mill, located near the Riverton line, was obtained from the Farmington River.[1] Unable to survive the Panic of 1857, Ward's Mill was forced to cease operation. A fire in 1890 destroyed the mill, but a new factory was built and used as a paper mill by John Ward's grandsons, William and George Ransbotham. In 1941, the site was damaged again by fire and the great flood of 1955 devastated what remained. Household cloth production remained somewhat longer in the Hartland area then in other sections of the state, and as a result of our Connecticut quilt documentation, we were fortunate to locate pieces that used fabrics from this mill.

Nellie L. Gates was born and raised in Riverton. She married George Ransbotham in 1892 when she was thirty-three years old and set up housekeeping in the town. Nellie and George had one son, Kenneth. He was not to live very long, as he died at the age of two with George Ransbotham dying three months after his son in 1895. The marriage had lasted only three years, leaving Nellie a widow at thirty-six. She never remarried.

According to family tradition, Nellie was taught to quilt by her mother at a very early age and made this Tumbling Block quilt in 1876 when she was seventeen years old. Nellie was the great-aunt of Edmund Holcomb, who is a direct descendant of John Ward. The quilt was handed down through the generations, along with the belief that some of the fabrics Nellie used were scraps obtained from Ward's Mill. Although the quilt was made a number of years after Ward's ceased operation, it was not unusual for fabric to be kept for a number of years before being used. The family possesses a swatch book, which contains fabrics similar to the ones found in Nellie's quilt.

Samples of fabric from Ward's Mill, c. 1836. Put together in a scrapbook by Nellie.

Tumbling Block,
c. 1876, made by
Nellie L. Gates
Ransbotham
(1859-1927),
Riverton,
cotton, 82" x 82".
Owned by Eloise
Holcomb
Henault,
daughter of
Edmund Joseph
Holcomb.

Ward's Mill

*I*n 1835, John Ward of North Adams, Massachusetts and his sons, Michael and James, purchased property in the southwestern section of Hartland. They built a calico factory and print works on a former sawmill site and opened the business as John Ward and Sons. When the calico factory began operation, it was the largest industry within Hartland's borders, and was one of the first in the United States to produce calico.

Log Cabin, Barn Raising Variation, c. 1865-1890, made by Emogene Cornelia Hayes Green (1856-1942), Granby, cotton, 79.5" x 79". Owned by Carla Bue. Emogene Cornelia Hayes Green was born in 1856 in East Granby and died in 1942. She married Carl Aaron Green (1856-1940) of Agawam, Massachusetts in 1879 at her family homestead, Bushy Hill, in Granby. They were the parents of seven children: six girls and one boy. The family farmed tobacco and traded horses. Their daughter, Helen Green, was the first woman to serve in the Connecticut legislature in 1926.
This quilt was made from fabrics from Ward's Mill in Hartland, is hand pieced and hand quilted, and in excellent condition.

Lone Star, c. 1865-1890, made by Eliza Miranda Allen Green (1835-1923), Gustavus, Ohio, cotton, 82" x 84". Owned by Carla Bue, Eliza's great-great-granddaughter. Eliza Miranda Allen was born in Gustavus, Ohio to Dr. Francis Allen and Eliza Goodrich Allen, natives of Granby, who migrated to Ohio. After the death of three of their children in one week during a cholera epidemic, the family returned to Granby. The family was further devastated with the loss of two sons in the Civil War. Eliza married Aaron Charles Green (1832-1898) of Wales, Massachusetts, in 1879 and they became the parents of three sons: Carl, John, and Frank. The Greens were active in their community, becoming founding members of the Granby Civic Club and the South Congregational Church. Eliza was involved in making charity quilts, some of which are now housed in the Salmon Brook Historical Society. Her quilt was made from fabrics from Ward's Mill in Hartland.

Sarah Elizabeth Allyn Latham

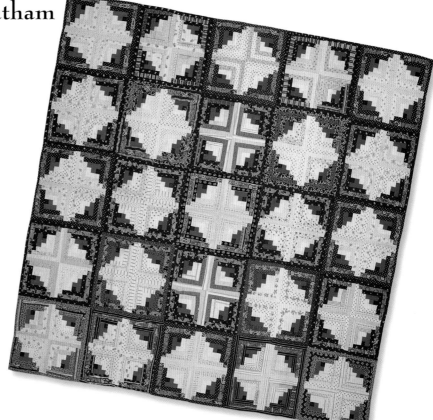

Log Cabin, Sunshine and Shadows Variation, c. 1865-1890, made by Sarah Elizabeth Allyn Latham (1839-1912), Gales Ferry, cotton, 91" x 91". Owned by Luella Daniels Landis.

*S*arah Elizabeth Allyn was the daughter of a seafaring captain and accompanied her parents on voyages to far and distant places. Sarah survived a shipwreck off the coast of Montauk, New York, when she was not quite eight years old. She attended the Music Vale Academy in Salem, Connecticut, where she honed her skills as a pianist. In 1865, Sarah married Thomas Latham and had four children.

Sarah's hand-pieced Log Cabin quilt was arranged in a Courthouse Steps pattern. She combined cotton and wool, and freely mixed solid colored fabrics with florals, paisleys, geometrics, and novelty prints of blue, brown, red, and ecru. Each of the one hundred blocks is nine and one-quarter inches square. The center of each block, commonly referred to as a "chimney," is traditionally red in color, but Sarah's quilt had red, white, and blue centers.

One of the things that makes this quilt special is its use of commemorative fabric for the backing. It is made of panels featuring the Memorial Hall Art Gallery. The United States celebrated its first century as a nation by hosting a Centennial Exhibition in Philadelphia, and Memorial Hall was especially constructed for this event. It connected directly with the Main Building to form the largest building in the world in 1876: it covered over twenty-one acres and was 936,008 square feet in size.[1] The United States erected exhibits featuring American artists and sculptors honoring our colonial history, and other nations were invited to exhibit artwork or industrial displays. The Exhibition lasted for a year and the Centennial themes caught the imagination of the American public. The Colonial Revival influence in architecture and interior design both date from this event.

This quilt has been passed down from mother to daughter for four generations. Sarah Allyn Latham died in 1912, and it is not clear if she gave the quilt to her daughter, Florence Latham Morgan, upon her death, or if Florence received it earlier. Florence passed the quilt on to her own daughter, Florence Morgan Daniels, who in turn gave it to daughter Luella Daniels Landis, the current owner. In the 1960s, Sarah's quilt won a blue ribbon in the 1965 Durham Fair.

The backing is panels of commemorative fabric featuring the Memorial Hall Art Gallery at the 1876 Centennial Exhibition in Philadelphia.

93

Gertrude Fyler Hotchkiss

The maker of this pristine silk appliqué Basket of Tulips quilt remains a mystery, but its association with a prominent Connecticut family continues to lure researchers.

Gertrude Fyler Hotchkiss was a notable Torrington philanthropist, remembered in her obituary for her "friendliness, kindness and generosity." When she died a childless widow at the age of eighty-eight in 1956, she left her entire estate, including her turn-of-the-century Main Street mansion to the Torrington Historical Society. Included in the contents of the estate was this quilt, which Torrington Historical Society records indicate belonged to Gertrude's grandmother, Sarah Bliss Vail (1819-1896). Sarah was married to David M. Vail, formerly of Cornwall, who had operated a carriage making shop there. He continued manufacturing carriages in Torrington upon their relocation. The quilt is made entirely by hand and is elaborately quilted with eleven stitches per inch. If this is the same silk quilt that she loaned to an 1897 exhibit, its planned destiny may have been re-routed.

In the course of research, the Torrington Historical Society uncovered a pamphlet for a spring 1897 YMCA exhibit in Torrington that listed as "loaned by Mrs. Gertrude Flyer Hotchkiss" a "Silk quilt, made for the Crystal Palace Exhibit at London, afterward to be presented to Queen Victoria: The Crystal Palace was burned before the quilt was completed. Cost of quilting, $25."

The first Crystal Palace Exhibition, an international event, was conceived by Queen Victoria's husband and held in 1851. Over five hundred of the exhibits were of American origin. After this first presentation, the magnificent building was dismantled and rebuilt at Sydenham Hall in South London, reopening in 1854. It remained the site of many exhibits and events. The specific Crystal Palace fire that the YMCA brochure refers to has not been determined at this time; Queen Victoria, however, to whom this quilt was to have been presented, died January 22, 1901. Although no one can say with absolute certainty that this is the same quilt loaned to the YMCA, it was the only silk quilt found in the contents of Gertrude's estate.

Gertrude was born on September 21, 1868, the daughter of Orasmus and Mary Vail Fyler. Her father, a Civil War veteran, was well known as Chairman of the Republican State Central Committee. In 1896, Gertrude married Edward Hotchkiss, who later became Chairman of the Board of the Hotchkiss Brothers Company, a successful family millwork and building company in Torrington. Their home, now known as the Hotchkiss-Fyler Museum, is open seasonally, and showcases both Gertrude's extensive collection of decorative arts and the fine millwork the company offered.

Besides her involvement in the Torrington Women's Club and the Charlotte Hungerford Hospital Auxiliary, Gertrude was also an avid gardener. She often opened her home and gardens for teas to benefit the Torrington Historical Society and many other organizations. Gertrude established a fund to provide Christmas gifts for children at the Cancer Memorial Center in New York City, now known as the Sloane-Kettering Cancer Institute. The fund still operates today as The Children's Joy Fund.

Basket of Tulips, c. 1865-1890, attributed to Gertrude Fyler Hotchkiss, Torrington, silk, 98" x 100". Owned by The Torrington Historical Society. *Photo by David Stansbury.*

The Universalist Social Benevolent Society

"Give my love to all Hartford. Especially the Sewing Circle."
—Cornelia B. Skinner[1]

An 1875 reference in the Church records contains the need to provide the first inside water closet in the history of Hartford Universalism. The accounts indicate that a "red and white bed quilt" raised $25 for this needed facility—members of the Church paid ten cents for each vote or signature.[2] It is uncertain whether this is the same red and white quilt. Most likely this quilt was made in 1882, in conjunction with the Ladies Society's 50th anniversary, known as "The Hartford Jubilee" or the State Convention. In addition to commemorating this event, it was announced that the church's $9,000 mortgage had been paid, thus releasing the church from debt. The 716 celebrants whose signatures appear on the quilt include ministers and members of churches from Norwich, Meriden, and Litchfield. Remarks were delivered at the celebration by P.T. Barnum and the Rev. C.A. Skinner.[3]

The ladies of this remarkable organization used their needlework skills to raise monies for everything from furnishing the church parlor to the minister's salary. In 1890, they made "16 mattress covers, 6 bed quilts and 26 comfortables."[4]

Sunflower Fundraising Quilt, c. 1865-1890, made by The Universalist Church of West Hartford, cotton, 87" x 87". Owned by The Universalist Church of West Hartford.

The Ladies Benevolent Association of the Second Ecclesiastical Society of Suffield

"Autograph Bedquilt."[5]

A few miles north of Hartford is the town of Suffield. In 1701, to accommodate the growing church society and religious revival, a second Meetinghouse needed to be built. Pew room was always a "delicate and difficult" issue to early New Englanders. The plain and simple Puritans gave way in regard to rank and wealth when seated in the Meetinghouse. The West Congregation Society was organized on November 10, 1743. The first church of West Suffield was erected the following year. The present church is actually the third church built in 1839 on the foundation of the second meetinghouse.[6]

In 1885, The Ladies Benevolent Association of the Second Ecclesiastical Society of Suffield also created a fundraising quilt. Although the reason for the fundraising has been lost, the organization's record book has a $84.40 deposit from the "contributions to the 'Autograph Bedquilt.' "[7] The church historian, Marjorie Phelan believes that monies were needed to enlarge the Meetinghouse with the addition of the Chapel Room. The new addition to the church was completed by 1897.

Signatories of this sunburst quilt were also church members. Material for the quilt was purchased on June 16, 1885. Mrs. H.S. Sheldon completed the first block on August 6, 1885, raising $3.60. A total of twenty-five women made blocks for the quilt and it was completed in January 1888.[8] Families who took part in this fundraising effort include those with names synonymous with the tobacco farmers of Suffield: the Austins, Sheldons, Spencers, and Loomises, in addition to 640 others.

Sunflower Fundraising Quilt, 1885, made by The Ladies Benevolent Association of the West
Suffield Congregational Church, cotton, 73" x 72". Owned by West Suffield Congregational Church.

"We Are All Crazy"

Danbury Hospital Quilt

In 1885, the ladies of Danbury proved the old adage "if you want a job done, give it to a woman." Their quest was to establish a hospital in Danbury, which had a population of approximately nineteen thousand. Prosperity and Danbury were synonymous and hatting was Danbury's claim to fame. In 1780, Zadoc Benedict made the first hats in his manufactory on Main Street. One hundred years later, in 1880, yearly production reached four and a half million hats, made by twenty-two manufacturers and three thousand workers within the city limits.[1] A suitable hospital for this thriving southwestern Connecticut town was long overdue. This need was best expressed by the Hon. Lyman D. Brewster four years later at the hospital's dedication services: "Every man should take a rib, and every city have a good hospital."[2]

James Montgomery Bailey, a noted Danbury resident, wrote, "Too much praise cannot be given to the women of Danbury for their hours of continuous thought, days and weeks of persistent labor."[3] Several women served on the initial Board, whose charge was to find a location for the hospital. Working through the physicians, the Lady Managers (as they were known) rallied support and called a public meeting in 1882. It was not until April 1885, however, that the first association was established and had acquired two buildings described as Queen Anne style cottages located on Crane Street. This first place for the care of the sick was opened April 27, 1885.[4] Dr. Todd, a hospital beneficiary, responded in writing to his invitation to the hospital's opening with "I feel like congratulating the ladies especially, and all friends of the institution, for the magnificent result of their undertaking. The way has been long and often times beset with discouragement, but a glorious end crowns their work."[5] He went on to applaud the Lady Managers and not their male colleagues for the successful completion of the hospital, calling it Danbury's "crowning glory."[6] These same Lady Managers solicited the fundraising efforts of women workers in the hat factories, both through subscriptions and fundraising events.

This Crazy quilt, with its embroidered outline of the first Danbury Hospital, is dated "*April 15 & 16, 1885.*" Made by the hat trimmers of the Soft Department at the Beckerle & Co., a Danbury hat factory, it was displayed as early as April 7, 1885 at the J.M. Ives Co. showroom in the town. There were actually two quilts made for the fair to raise monies for the new hospital. The first had already been on exhibit at J.M. Ives Co. The sixteen hundred chances on that quilt sold out so quickly that a second quilt was made to accommodate the demand. A *Newstimes* article from April 2 reported about the second quilt: "This quilt is handsomer even than the other, and that is saying a great deal. One of the pieces is an outline view of the hospital building. On another is the date of the fair and festival. It is a remarkable piece of needlework."[7] It was raffled at a fair and sociable given by the hat trimmers of the Soft Department of Beckerle & Co. "Each and every lady has made something for the occasion, making it a very interesting collection of articles to be displayed, besides the two large quilts of crazy work."[8] The fair and sociable was held at Wildman's Hall on Wednesday, April 15 and 16, and raised $500 for the new hospital. It was written in the *Newstimes*: "The fair opened last night under most favorable circumstances. The hall was thronged with visitors the entire evening, and the scene was an animated one. The walls were decorated with buntings, and flags and suspended over and between the two handsome crazy-work quilts."[9] Mrs. J. A. Nobles was the winner of the second crazy quilt with the Danbury Hospital image.[10]

The quilt was made of scraps from silk hat linings. As befits good Yankee women who waste not, the trimmers used these castaway silk pieces as the foundation for their embroidered stitches. One can only guess at the meaning of "*We Are All Crazy*" embroidered in shiny thread near the center of the quilt. Perhaps that was the popular reaction among the men of the community to the persistence of the Danbury women to want to care for the sick. It may have been a critique or comment about the speed with which this

quilt was embroidered to meet the demands of the raffle ticket takers. Whatever the meaning, the quilt helped fund Danbury's greatest charity: its community hospital, or, as Dr. Todd stated, "its crowning glory."[11]

The crazy quilt is just one example of the spirit of cohesiveness and cooperation that the hat trimmers of Danbury embodied. This group of women would once again demonstrate their concerns in correcting society's injustices and inequalities. Their social consciousness would further distinguish themselves and cement their place in history. In 1887, shortly after this quilt was made, the trimmers were to form one of the first unions in the United States. In an effort to improve their salaries, working conditions, and the terms of their employment with fourteen hat manufactories, they held a lockout. It took place from November 17, 1890 to December 6, 1890, and was to be the very first union strike held anywhere in the United States.[12]

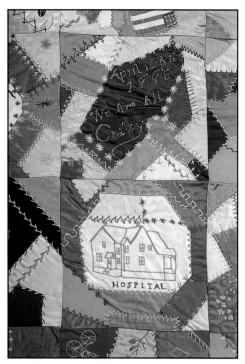

This is believed to be the only existing image of the first Danbury Hospital.

Crazy Quilt, April 15 & 16, 1885, made by the hat trimmers of the Soft Department of
Beckerle & Co., Danbury, silk, 57" x 66". Owned by The Dorothy Whitfield Historic Society.

Lucretia Norton Carlisle Tuttle

Lucretia Norton, born on April 19, 1820 to one of Goshen's founding families, left us with many treasurers from her life. Granddaughter Alice Carlisle presented them to the Goshen Historical Society for the generations to appreciate. These items include not only the two nineteenth-century quilts shown here, but also Lucretia's "quilting candle," Lucretia photographed in a white Victorian carriage, and her hand-painted fireboard.

Lucretia's vocation in life was to be a teacher, and her family had the means to enable her to attend the Goshen Academy in the center of town. In 1837, at the age of seventeen, Lucretia traveled with eight friends to teach in Greensborough, Alabama. Her journey took her first to Brookfield, then by stage to Norwalk. From there she boarded a boat to New York City, a ferry to New Jersey, and then rode the remaining distance to Alabama in a "carryall." In Alabama, she was intrigued by the log cabins of the South: "In this country some of the most wealthy people live in the most miserable log cabins." She described dining in one of the more luxurious cabins with two rooms: it was a "first rate place, the moon shone on the table very beautifully."[1]

Lucretia soon met her future husband, Elihu Carlisle of Marion, Alabama. On April 4, 1838, she recorded in her diary,

"Mr. C. wrote to father." Lucretia married Elihu Carlisle in her hometown of Goshen on July 28, 1840, and they returned to Alabama to make their home. They had two children, Caroline Susan on April 29, 1841 and Elihu on December 19, 1847. Sadly, her daughter died at the age of seven in 1848 and her husband died two years later in 1851. The painted fireboard is a bittersweet but cherished memory of her life and home in Alabama. It depicts a garden graced with flowers and beauty, but also the shrines of her husband and child.

Lucretia Carlisle returned home to Goshen with young Elihu. After the appropriate time of mourning, on October 2, 1854, she married Samuel B. Tuttle, formerly of Hartford. In 1855, she officially joined the church of her childhood, the First Congregational Church of Goshen.[2] Together, Samuel and Lucretia settled in Goshen where they raised Elihu and their daughter, Caroline Lucretia. Both children married in the 1870s, which is about the time her three quilts were made. It is possible the quilts were part of her daughter's or her son's hope chest. Caroline lived with her husband in Alabama and Elihu spent his years in Goshen Center. His daughter, Alice Carlisle, bequeathed this quilt treasury to the Goshen Historical Society.

The painted fireboard is a bittersweet, but cherished memory of Lucretia's home and life in Alabama.

This tin candleholder with its square base is identified by the family as Lucretia's "quilting candle."

Lucretia Norton Carlisle Tuttle seated in a white wicker carriage, Goshen.

Detail of the fireboard, showing Lucretia's Alabama home.

Another detail, showing the grave sites of her husband, Elihu, and her daughter, Caroline Susan.

Log Cabin with Fan Border, Jan. 20, 1885, made by Lucretia Norton Carlisle Tuttle, silk, 55" x 62". Owned by the Goshen Historical Society.

Nine-Patch, 1888, made by Lucretia Norton Carlisle Tuttle, silk, 51" x 67". Owned by the Goshen Historical Society.

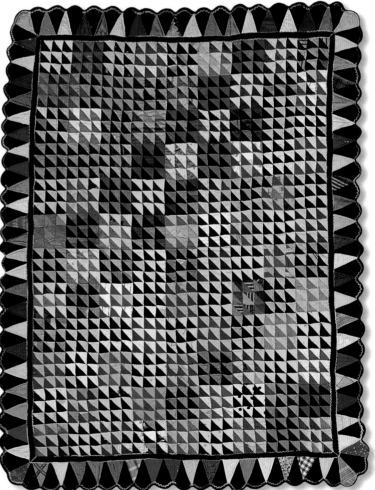

Emma Tracy Baldwin Gold

*I*t was November 1888, and Emma Gold had completed her Connecticut State quilt that was going to be presented at the 4th Annual State Grange meeting in Meriden. Begun in 1886, this quilt had become a priority for Emma. Her four children were grown, her three step-daughters were married and on their own, and she had the time to finish this beautiful quilt.

Emma Tracy was born in 1835, the daughter of Andrew W. Tracy and Emmaline Talcott Tracy. One of four children, Emma was born and grew up in the busy manufacturing town of Rockville, named after the Rock Factory, the first operating textile mill in the area. By 1835, the year Emma was born, there were six textile mills, one paper mill, one grist and saw mill, a shoe store, and one dry goods store. In 1838, the population numbered about three hundred and Rockville was an established mill community with multiple textile mills and mill owned housing.[1] By 1841, a post office was established.

Emma married Charles Baldwin of Cornwall, most likely in 1852, as an album of remembrances owned by her grandson contains several inscriptions dated 1852.

Unfortunately, the marriage was not a long one, as Charles died in 1858. There were no children from this marriage. On April 4, 1859 Emma married Theodore Sedgwick Gold, I, the son of Dr. Samuel Wadsworth and Pheobe Cleveland Gold. Theodore's first wife, Caroline Lockwood, had died in 1857 at age thirty-two, leaving three children; Eleanor, age fifteen, Rebecca, age eight, and Caroline, age four. Upon her marriage, not only did Emma instantly become a mother, but she also assumed the role of running a household which included Theodore's parents, and numerous students enrolled in the private agricultural school run by Theodore and his father.

Theodore was born in Madison, New York in 1818 and moved with his family to Goshen, Connecticut in 1824. He attended Goshen Academy, graduated from Yale in 1838, taught school in Goshen and Waterbury, and settled in Cornwall in 1842 as a farmer. In 1845, he and his father established the Cream Hill Agricultural School, which continued successfully for twenty-four years until 1869. It was considered to be among the best in New England.

During the next few years Emma's four children were born: Alice Tracy in 1860, Martha Wadsworth in 1861, Charles Lockwood in 1863, and James Douglas in 1866. In addition to the responsibilities of motherhood for her own four children and three stepchildren, Emma incorporated the responsibilities of overseeing from eight to twenty young men during the academic year. These students of the school lived in a dormitory attached to the main house and participated in all the Gold family activities, including meals. Emma oversaw and coordinated all of the operations of this large household.[2]

Cream Hill Agricultural School was an early version of today's prep schools. Students came from all over and many continued on to college, primarily attending Yale in New Haven. Not only were they instructed in agriculture and horticulture, they were also given lessons in Greek, French, algebra, chemistry, philosophy, astronomy, logic, geology, Spanish, German, punctuality, and behavior. Students were required to cultivate a vegetable garden plot of one hundred square yards, the fruits of which contributed to the fare provided to all inhabitants of Cream Hill. The Gold's daughters and neighborhood girls attended the same elective drawing classes as the boys, and doubtless were among the partners at the occasional dancing classes.

When the school closed in 1869, Theodore was involved in the Connecticut Agricultural Society. He was a trustee of the orphanage established at Storrs for Civil War orphans, and was a founder and trustee of the agricultural school established on its site, which eventually evolved into the University of Connecticut.[3] It was during these years that Emma made the quilt we so admire today.

Each of Connecticut's eight counties are pieced in a different color. Herring-bone stitches mark the county borders, and other stitches mark the lines of each of Connecticut's 169 towns. All ponds, rivers, and lakes are outlined in blue stitching. Major railroads are identified with black stitching. Connecticut's famous Charter Oak is depicted in white and the state seal is done in gold and green. The capital city of Hartford is designated with a star, and other major Connecticut cities are marked by small x's. Emma even identified her home—Cream Hill in Cornwall.

Descendants of Emma and Theodore still reside at the family homestead in Cornwall. Theodore died in 1906 at the age of eighty-eight. Emma died in 1927 at the age of ninety-two and they are both buried in the North Cornwall Cemetery.

Mrs Emma (Tracy) Gold

Emma Tracy Baldwin Gold

State of Connecticut, c. 1886, made by Emma Tracy Baldwin Gold (1835-1926), Cornwall, silk and satin, 69" x 59". Owned by the Gold Family.

The Gold Homestead at Cream Hill in Cornwall.

Ann Elizabeth Morehouse Prindle

Ann Elizabeth Morehouse Prindle lived her entire life of ninety-three years in the northwestern town of Sharon. Upon her death in March 1952, she was memorialized as Sharon's "Aunt Anna." *The Lakeville Journal* remembered her as "the dear little lady of a Victorian generation, loved for her clear reminiscences as well as her wit and gracious charm."[1]

Her life spanned a by-gone era of privilege and refinement enjoyed by Sharon's landed gentry. She was born on August 26, 1858 to Julius and Elizabeth Denison Morehouse. Ann Elizabeth was the fifth of eight children born into this successful farming family. She was a fourth generation Morehouse to be born and live in Bogardus Hall.

Ann attended school at the Amenia Seminary in New York. During her years there, the school had up to 247 students with a library of over 1,600 volumes.[2] Her formal education ended at the age of seventeen in order to assist her parents, whose health was failing. She assumed the household duties at Bogardus Hall. Her activities included making barrels of soap, candles, putting up preserves, jams, and jellies. She made the family's sheets, over 110 yards of rag carpet, and quilts for all.

Ann would have been just thirteen years of age when her parents celebrated their 25th wedding anniversary in December 1871. One of her favorite stories was of the momentous event. There were six hundred people invited to the gala, which also served as the "inauguration of their palatial residence." *The Harlem Valley Times* reported on December 14, 1871: "The house was swarming with humanity from ground floor to garret." The Hon. John Cotton Smith, the Governor of Connecticut, was a family friend and special guest. Ann recalled in her later years being twirled around the dance floor by the head of the state of Connecticut so fast that "the only way I could keep up with his long legs was to grab onto his coattails and hang on for dear life."[3] Fabric from the dress Ann wore that night was one of her treasures. Years later, she included its scraps in one of her Mariner's Compass quilts.

The Mariner's Compass pattern was Ann's all-time favorite pattern. She made at least sixteen quilts with that design. She took orders from neighbors eager to own her quilts. She always had compass points cut and ready in her scrap bag, awaiting the right matching or coordinating fabric to finish her next quilt. She made just one other quilt pattern, a Friendship quilt, made from material given to her by friends. Her sister, Julia, penned their names in the blocks' centers "in a fine Spencerian hand."[4] As Ann aged, her sight began to fail but her love for quilting remained constant. To assist her, friends and relatives would bring her pincushions of pre-threaded needles ready to stitch.

Ann's spinster life changed with the death of her sister, Julia Rebecca, on August 8, 1921. Julia had been married to Charles Mark Prindle of Sharon for nearly fifty years. Together they had six children. Sixteen months after Julia's death, Ann and Charles were married on December 14, 1922, at the Episcopal Church in Sharon.

Ann was sixty-four years of age when they wed. They shared sixteen years together before Charles's death in 1938. As some of the longest living residents of the area, Charles and Ann were frequently asked to reconstruct Sharon's past for the local *Lakeville Journal*. Ann remained active in her community as a devoted Episcopalian and a loyal member of the Republican Party. Only once did she defy her family's staunch Republican support by announcing her vote for Franklin Delano Roosevelt. It was said that Aunt Anna "could hold her own in argument for F.D.R."[5]

Ann Elizabeth Morehouse Prindle died on March 21, 1952 at the age of ninety-three. Fifty years later it is possible that only two of her Mariner's Compass quilts remain. This one is in the possession of the Sharon Historical Society on the Sharon Green. The other has been passed to her great niece, Mrs. Joan C. Scribner Bettman, of Chapel Hill, North Carolina.

Opposite page: Mariner's Compass, 1887, made by Ann Elizabeth Morehouse Prindle (1858-1952), Sharon, cotton, 74" x 96". Owned by The Sharon Historical Society. *Photo by David Stansbury.*

Ann Elizabeth Morehouse Prindle with her nieces, c. 1949. *Photo courtesy of Mrs. Betty Morehouse Scribner.*

105

Nella Babcock Bradford

Nella Babcock was born to a farming family in the community of Plainfield. In addition to its cotton and woolen factories on the Quinnebaug River, Plainfield's fertile soil, which produced an abundance of corn, brought it the affectionate designation of "Egypt."[1] As the oldest daughter of William S. and Frances E. Babcock, Nella learned all of the traditional female duties to keep a large household going.

Educated at the Plainfield Academy, Nella became a teacher in Canterbury. She made her highly decorated Crazy quilt most likely in preparation for her marriage in 1890 to George Bradford from Canterbury. Dated June 1889, it includes all of the popular floral and garden motifs of the era. Family history tells us that the center silk circle was from the top hat of her father, William Babcock. She further embellished it with her own ornamental embroidered daisies and forget-me-nots.

George served in the Connecticut Legislature as a Representative from Canterbury.[2] He was also a successful farmer, blacksmith, and carpenter. Nella was an astute businesswoman who made sixty pounds of butter every other day and delivered it to Danielson. In 1906, while building a new home in Plainfield, George died unexpectedly. Nella moved her three children, Alice, John, and Cecil, to Plainfield and supported the family through various business and farming ventures. All three children completed high school and two finished college. The quilt, a cherished family heirloom, was passed down through the family and belongs to a great-granddaughter.

1890 Marriage Certificate for Nella Babcock and George Bradford.

Nella Babcock Bradford

106

Crazy Quilt, 1889, made by Nella Babcock Bradford, Plainfield, velvet and silk, 64" x 64.5". Owned by Ann Anderberg.

Laura Electa Seymour

Laura Electa Seymour

Laura Electa Seymour was born in New Hartford and was only two years of age when her parents moved to Bristol. Educated in the local schools and the Mr. J. W. J. Curtis' Boarding and Day School in Hartford, she pursued a teaching profession. Like her sisters, she was interested in social matters and was remembered as being very charitable. The Seymour sisters, Laura, Mary, and Grace, were regarded in Bristol's high society as women who gave "more tone to its society, which they enriched by their high breeding, their cultivation and their Christian principles, than any three women who ever lived in it."[1]

On November 1, 1876, Laura E. Seymour signed her name in the visitors' book at the great 1876 Centennial Exhibition in Philadelphia. She was one of forty thousand Connecticut residents to attend this testimonial celebration of the Centennial birthday of the United States. Her sister, Grace, had been there on October 19 and her father attended on November 9. While there, Laura purchased the four fabric panels depicting the Horticulture Hall, Machinery Hall, the Art Gallery, and the Main Building. The National Water-Wheel Company, one of the Seymour business interests, represented the single Bristol exhibit. It was also one of the Connecticut companies to receive an award of accommodation.[2]

Laura Leggett Seymour was Laura Electa's first niece and the daughter of her brother, Henry. Born on November 11, 1873, in Washington, D.C., she was nearly three years old when her Aunt Laura attended the Centennial. The child-size quilt incorporates the four panels of the Exhibition on one side and nine scenes from children's literature surrounded by red fabric on the reverse side. Aunt Laura's quilt symbolized many of the important interests in her life that she hoped to pass onto her niece: her love of flowers, reading, art, and her family's business.

Laura Electa's life spanned Bristol's most prosperous economic years in the nineteenth century, when the clock industry dominated the manufacturing scene. She lived her entire life in the family's home at No. 37 Prospect Place. Sadly, she became deaf, finding her only solitude in the study of flowers and birds. She died in her home on June 22, 1922 after a long illness.[3]

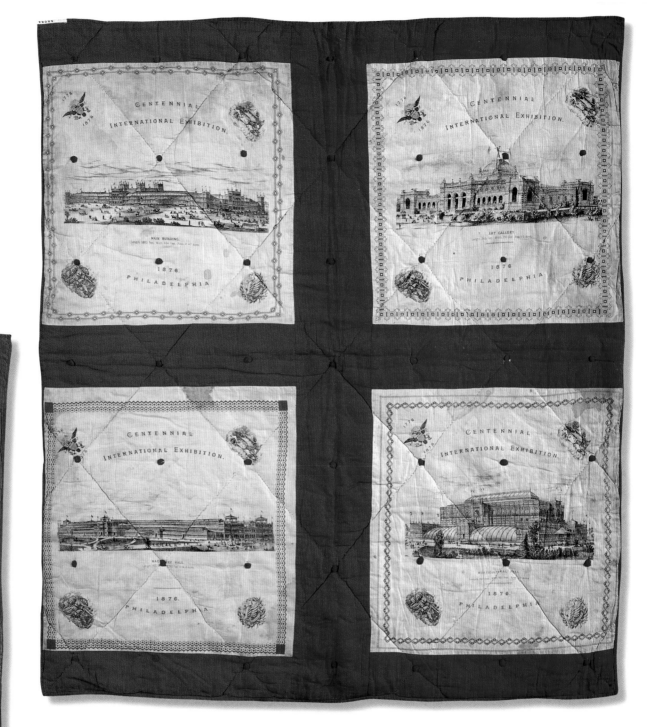

Commemorative, c. 1865-1890, made by Laura Electa Seymour (1846-1922), Bristol, cotton, 46.5" x 52". Owned by the New Haven Colony Historical Society. Fabric panels depicting Horticulture Hall, Machinery Hall, the Art Gallery, and the Main Building of the 1876 Centennial Exhibition in Philadelphia. *Photo by David Stansbury.*

Back of the quilt has fabric scenes from children's literature. *Photo by David Stansbury.*

109

Susan Hill Buck

The time-honored Nine-Patch quilt was documented in abundance in a number of variations among the nineteenth-century quilts of Connecticut. Susan Hill Buck's quilt is one of the best representations of this popular pattern. Arranged in a straight set with an alternating plain block, the 140 pieced squares with their bountiful array of scraps create a bright and colorful quilt. To set off her fabric gem, Susan Hill Buck added a three-sided swag border enhanced with a bow at the peak of each swag. It is easy to believe that the happy colors reflected Susan's own vibrant personality, since she is remembered as a woman of "ability and activity" with a "remarkable interest in all things."[1]

Susan's hometown of New Milford was and still is the shopping center for many of the more rural towns in its surrounds. A journal written by Ella Pierce of Roxbury in 1877 makes many references to shopping trips there and her purchases of threads and yard goods including calico. The first calico was said to have been available in New Milford in 1804.[2]

In 1814, New Milford was described in the *State Gazetteer of Connecticut* as a "large and flourishing town." Its population of 3,537 in 1810 boasted sixteen schools. Still primarily a farming community, the town also had numerous mills and manufactories. Among those were a woolen factory, a hat factory, four carding mills, six fulling mills, and four tanneries. The village had seven mercantile stores.[3]

After Susan and David Marsh Buck married in 1837, they settled on a farm south of the village of New Milford. Samuel Buck, the author of *Origin, History and Genealogy of the Buck Family*, recalls visiting their farm and the nearby old Buck homestead, where David's cousin Theodore and his family resided. Samuel Buck stated:

> Both families were relatives whom we visited in 1860 and 1861. The first settlements were upon the hillsides overlooking the valley or village which they seemed to prefer for various reasons of Outlook, water, pasturage, fuel, security air and healthiness.[4]

Susan's long life spanned most of the nineteenth century and just into the beginning of the twentieth century. Blessed with three children, Mary Ann, Jane Althea, and Joseph Leroy, Susan and David raised their family in New Milford near the banks of the Housatonic River. Devote Episcopalians, Susan and David may have been one of the first young couples to be married in the new Episcopal Church constructed on the Green in 1837. The Green in those days was still a compound where cattle, horses, swine, sheep, and fowl could be held.[5]

Susan Hill Buck lived to be over ninety years and was predeceased by her daughters. Her obituary states that:

> ...death came suddenly after an illness of only two days and in its quiet peace seemed verily an entering into rest. Mrs. Buck was for many years a member and zealous worker in St. John's church of which her husband was at one time Warden. Devoted to her home and family, ever ready to lend a hand to friends in need, she will be remembered always with love and reverence. So few are given so great a number of years of ability and activity; for to the last she retained a remarkable interest in all things and exceptional vitality; ever one of her strongest characteristics.[6]

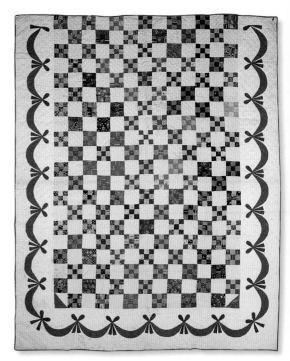

Nine-Patch, c. 1865-1890, made by Susan Hill Buck (1814-1904), New Milford, cotton, 85" x 104". Owned by New Milford Historical Society.

1838 Painting of Aspetuck Hill, New Milford, featuring the white steeple of the Episcopal Church. Painting by William Jewett. *Courtesy of New Milford Historical Society.*

Mrs. K. H. Colvin

This full size quilt appears to be an original design of appliquéd flowers in a medallion arrangement. A bouquet of lilies springs from the center with rosebuds beneath it. An oval wreath of rosebuds and grapes encircle the lilies.

The Colvin family lived in the small eastern town of Brooklyn in the 1800s. Mrs. K.H. Colvin presented this quilt to Dilla May Cady Evans on September 22, 1885. Dilla was married to Elisha Evans, who sold livestock in the area and was also in the lumber business. Dilla gave the quilt to Susie E. Andrews on May 3, 1891, who in 1894 married Dilla and Elisha's son, Henry Evans. Henry worked as a butcher as well as a farmer. He and Susie had two children: Walter, born on March 28, 1896, and Edith May, born on December 6, 1898. After Walter married Dorris Fitzgerald on September 30, 1922, the quilt was given to him by his mother.

This quilt never left the small town of its origin, and has passed quietly through the generations with many families enjoying its beauty. The quilt currently belongs to Walter and Dorris's youngest child.

Appliquéd Lilies, 1885, made by Mrs. K.H. Colvin, Brooklyn, cotton, 71" x 85". Owned by Margaret Evans Traskos.

The Bunnell Family

Harriett Burdict Farnsworth (1810-1897)
Caroline Lowrey Bunnell (1814-1893)
Almira Phoebe Farnsworth Bunnell
  (1839-1926)
Mamre Anne Bunnell (1871-1952)

*N*ovelist and poet, Mrs. Sarah Hale, better known as editor of *Godey's Lady's Book*, spent thirty years trying to convince government officials, including several different presidents, to consider the value of a national Thanksgiving Day. Sarah had an idea that "a national holiday would unify the country, and draw it together in common bonds of prayer and gratitude."[1] Her earnest solicitations won the attention of Abraham Lincoln and in 1863 he issued a proclamation for a national Thanksgiving Day, which is still celebrated today.

It was on this thankful holiday in 1896 that the Bunnell family gathered together for the family portrait shown here. Their house on 13 Stafford Avenue in the Forestville section of Bristol was extremely large with clapboard siding, shuttered windows, and a side porch. The family homestead of William Edwin Bunnell and Almira P. Farnsworth Bunnell was bequeathed to William by his father, Edwin, with the provision that his sister Charity (1802-1884) would always have a home there. Also living there were the six children of William and Almira (which included two sets of twins), William's mother, Caroline, and Almira's mother, Harriet.

This family's biography depicts late nineteenth-century life in Bristol, a working class town with a strong industrial base. Family members recall Almira and her daughter Mamre as quiltmakers, but also remembered that the other women in the house participated as well. They apparently worked well together as is evidenced by these examples of their home industry. The Courthouse Steps quilt reflects the practical habits of Connecticut women: "waste not, want not." The creative use of fabric scraps in each of the eighty-one, nine-inch blocks form red "H" centers between the blended light and dark fabrics. In the eight-pointed star, three dozen scrap fabrics are set on point and held to their backing with simple outline hand quilting. The stars, separated by one-and-a-half inch

sashing strips, appear to float on the field of muslin. Several other quilts from this household were sold at auction when Mamre died in 1952 and others remain with family members, including a

Grandmother's Flower Garden quilt made by Mamre. While it is not clear who made the quilts pictured here, it is evident that quiltmaking in this family was truly a family affair.

Eight Pointed Star, c. 1865-1890, made by the Bunnell Family, Bristol, cotton, 77" x 83". Owned by Jean F. Joseph.

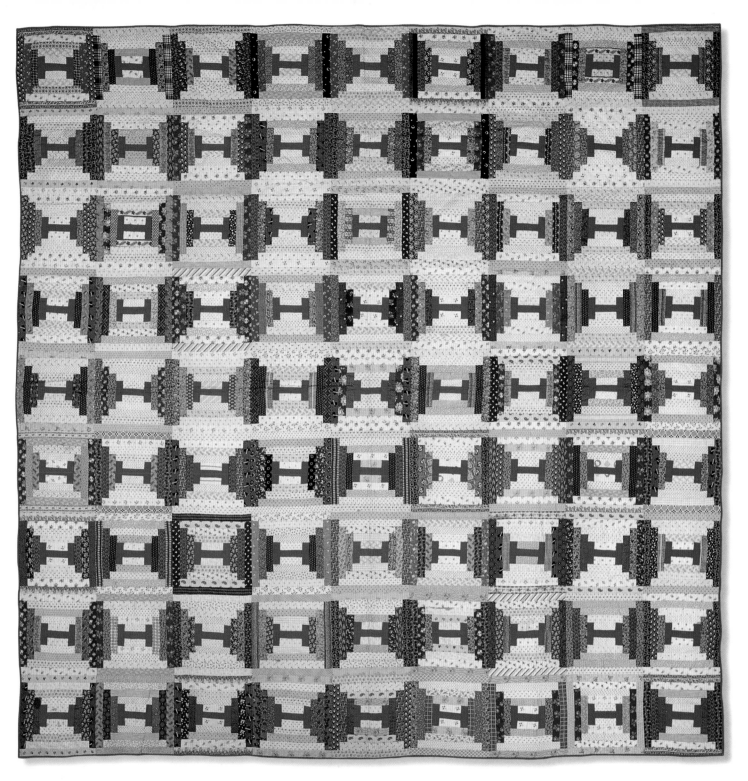

Log Cabin, Courthouse Steps Variation, c. 1890-1925, made by the Bunnell
Family, Bristol, cotton, 85.5" x 85.5". Owned by Jean F. Joseph.

Opposite page, bottom:
The Bunnell family of Bristol celebrated Thanksgiving Day in 1896 by having a
family photograph taken. Back row: Carlton Lowery, Carrie Louise Bond (Carlton's
wife), Maude Almira, Mamre Anne, Edwin Solomon, Caroline Edna. Middle row:
William Edwin, Harriet (Burdict) Farnsworth (Almira's mother), Almira Phoebe.
Front row: Hazel Jennet, William Carlton.

113

The Morgan Sisters' Quilt

Flora Drew Morgan and her sister, Laura Fairchild Morgan, were born and raised in the town of Bethel in the 1860s. They were the daughters of Sally Drew Morgan and Caleb Morgan. The family's farm was located at Morgan Heights where it branched out of Putnam Park. Their mother's family emigrated from England during the Revolutionary War period. The sisters never married and both died between 1930 and 1940.

Laura, also known as Dora, did not work for pay, but Flora worked in a hat factory in Danbury, known as "The Hat City." According to family tradition, Flora brought home scraps of silk fabrics, which were used to line hats. A number of Connecticut mills produced silk cloth used for hat linings, and many companies took advantage of the popularity of crazy quilts to sell their scraps.[1]

This stunning example of a crazy quilt is almost perfectly square. It is made of satin, velvet, and silk scraps, and is embellished with paintings, beads, ribbon work, sequins, and embroidery. A variety of embroidery stitches were used to outline the blocks, which feature flowers, fans, crescent moons, stars, leaves, and chenille work of a sumac plant. A four-inch, crocheted lace edging surrounds this magnificent quilt. It was made as a gift for Edward J. Morgan, president of the machine company, Coulter & McKenzie, in Bridgeport, and was passed down to his granddaughter.

Flora Drew Morgan and her sister, Laura Fairchild Morgan.

Crazy Quilt, c. 1875-1910, made by Flora Drew Morgan and Laura Fairchild Morgan,
Bethel, satin, velvet, and silk, 74" x 75". Owned by Eleanor H. Smith.

Remarkable embroidery
stitching adorns this quilt.

Woman's Relief Corps

These two quilts made eleven years apart are historical documents that provide evidence of the benevolent work of the Woman's Relief Corps (WRC) and the generous support of a manufacturing town. They span the time when Bristol changed from a small rural village to an enterprising modern city. Many of the names on the quilts reflect the names of Bristol streets, schools, and businesses.

The Woman's Relief Corps, a national organization whose motto was Fraternity, Charity and Loyalty, was the Allied Order of the Grand Army of the Republic (GAR), a Civil War Veterans' Association. The GAR, also a national organization, consisted of men who fought for the Union during the Civil War. They founded soldiers' homes and were not only active in relief work, but also politically active in pension legislation. The GAR and the WRC were responsible for the institution of Memorial Day and the standardization of the Pledge of Allegiance that we recite today.

Gilbert W. Thompson WRC # 4 of Bristol, Connecticut, was the fourth department to be organized in the state of Connecticut in 1883. They provided the programs and the decorations for patriotic days, hospitality for civic events, performed relief work for veterans and their families, and bought grave markers for soldiers' graves. To raise funds for their work, the women sponsored events that not only brought cash for their treasury, but entertainment for the town.

In 1885, a great celebration was held to commemorate Bristol's 100th year as a town. The Centennial festivities included the Great Loan Exhibit, which displayed items from the past. Each display area consisted of antiquities relating to a specific category, such as farm implements, domestic life and manufacturing. However, the ladies of the WRC had another idea, which was chronicled by John J. Jennings:

One of the most unique schemes for aiding the Grand Army, is that represented by a large, though incomplete, bed-quilt hanging on the east side. In the center are the badges of Gilbert W. Thompson Post, GAR, and the Ladies' Relief Corps, No. 4. Every third block - all the blocks being three inches long by one wide - is white, on each of which Miss Keziah Peck, of the Corps, has written in indelible ink the name of some person who has paid a dime for that purpose. The ladies have done all the sewing. There are now nearly seven hundred names on the quilt, which is to be finished in time for their fair next winter. The blocks are red, white, and blue.[1]

Signature Quilt, 1896, made by members of the Woman's Relief Corps, Bristol, cotton, 77" x 87.5". Owned by the Bristol Historical Society. Made to commemorate the 1896 Annual State Convention marked by the attendance of Past National President, Emma R. Wallace. Over four hundred names were signed with pencil and then embroidered with red floss. Each block was organized in an orderly design remindful of corps discipline. Besides Bristol corps members, other Bristol supporters appear on the quilt along with the names of other local organizations that shared the use of the GAR meeting hall. Considering the nature of the WRC, it is reasonable to conclude that this quilt was also used as a fundraiser.

Rail Fence, 1885, made by members of the Woman's Relief Corps, Bristol, cotton, 80" x 78". Owned by the Bristol Historical Society. Nearly seven hundred members paid a dime to have their names inscribed on this fundraising quilt.

Celina Gagnon LaBonne

Celina Gagnon LaBonne

Celina Gagnon was born in Les Trois Pistols, Canada, on August 15, 1875, the daughter of Xavier and Marie Pelletier Gagnon. Xavier made his livelihood riding logs on the St. Lawrence River. It was a dangerous and not always rewarding job. Word spread about all the mills being built in the United States and the money that could be made there, so the Gagnons packed up their belongings and moved to Jewett City, Connecticut to find work in one of the many textile factories.

When Celina was only nine years old, she left school to work twelve-hour days in the local mill. As she matured, she eventually apprenticed as a pattern maker and a dressmaker, which became her trade until she married. The forest green dress in the portrait was styled and sewn by Celina.

On October 16, 1900, Celina married George LaBonne. George, also a Canadian, was born in LaBonneville, Canada, on March 26, 1875. He was a butcher, later advancing to become a store manager. Celina and George quickly settled into married life and had nine children: six sons and three daughters. The family attended the Roman Catholic church. Celina made a christening gown for her first child, George T., born January 17, 1902, and all family members since have worn that gown. In 1908, the LaBonnes moved to Waterbury and spent the rest of their lives there. Celina died in the early 1940s and George died in 1955.

This pristine Log Cabin, Barn Raising variation, has sixty-four pieced blocks, all with orange centers floating among multi-colored scraps. It is believed she saved the scraps from her mill job. The backing is cotton chintz printed with apple blossoms. It is quilted with peach-colored thread at five stitches to the inch.

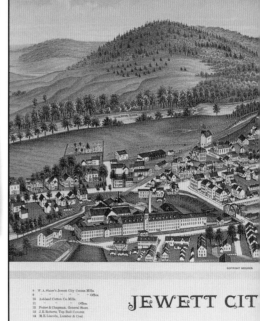

Log Cabin, Barn Raising Variation, c. 1895, made by Celina Gagnon LaBonne, Jewett City, velvet, 75" x 77". Owned by Lois LaBonne Hanlon. This pristine quilt has sixty-four pieced blocks, all with orange centers floating among the multi-colored scraps. The backing is cotton chintz printed with apple blossoms. Unlike many Log Cabin quilts, this one is quilted, not tied, using a peach-colored thread with five stitches per inch.

Medallion, c. 1895-1900, made by Celina Gagnon LaBonne, Waterbury, velvet, 45" round. Owned by Lois LaBonne Hanlon. Celina's striking table cover was obviously intended to be displayed. The round 45" diameter Victorian tablecloth is made of velvet scraps stitched to a foundation. The cloth is multi-colored, but gold and maroon are predominant. Diamond-shaped pieces create a star in the center of the cloth that radiates out to the individual diamonds that encircle the outer edges of the work. By using a wide range of decorative embroidery stitches to further ornament the surface, Celina was able to display her admirable talents. Both of these pieces are owned by the quiltmaker's oldest granddaughter.

Detail from an 1889 L.R. Burleigh map.

119

Octavia Harvey Royce

*P*erhaps living her life in a place called Rainbow, a small village in Windsor, offset the many hardships that life brought to Octavia Harvey Royce. It was after the Civil War that Octavia married Charles Royce. He had been with the 16th Regiment of the Connecticut Volunteers. Badly injured, he received an early discharge and was disabled for the rest of his life. Their only child, Mildred Octavia Royce, was born in 1872.

As contributing members of their community, Octavia and Charles were involved in the Congregational Church and the Masonic Lodge. Octavia was the main wage earner in her family, working in the local post office. Their daughter Mildred married Charles Lidstedt and started her own family. By the end of the nineteenth century, their contented lives were about to

take a turn. Charles Royce died in February 1899 at the age of fifty-five. Only four months later, a granddaughter died at the age of four years and only two years after that, Mildred, her dear daughter, and another grandson also were gone.

Quilts are made for many reasons. Working through grief is one very real reason for a woman to pick up a needle and create a beautiful memorial. The velvets, silks, and satins of Octavia's quilt and sham are adorned with commemorative ribbons from Charles's days with the 16th Conn. Volunteers' reunion in 1896 and a ribbon marking the dedication of the new State House.

Octavia lived out her life with her son-in-law and grandson at their home in East Hartford and it is certain that she treasured her quilts until her death in 1938.

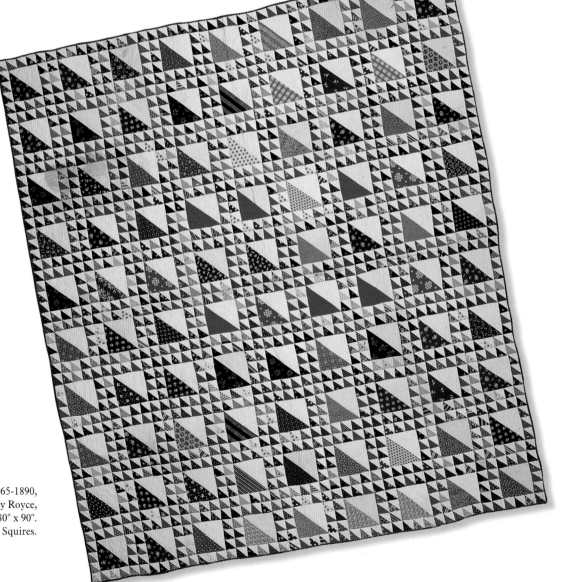

Lady of the Lakes, c. 1865-1890,
made by Octavia Harvey Royce,
East Hartford, cotton, 80" x 90".
Owned by Elizabeth P. Squires.

Log Cabin, Pineapple Variation, c. 1875, made by Octavia Harvey Royce, East Hartford, satin and silk, 70" x 70". Owned by Elizabeth P. Squires.

Crazy Quilt, 1896, made by Octavia Harvey Royce, East Hartford, satin and silk, 21" x 21". Owned by Elizabeth P. Squires.

Myra Lord Converse

The town of Stafford Springs, located in the northeastern section of Connecticut, is situated at the head-waters of the Willimantic River. It has been home to several important mills, some of which are still in existence. Stafford was settled in 1719 on land formerly used by the Nipmuck Indian Tribe. The native inhabitants discovered the medicinal values of the springs as they camped along several streams. During this time, Stafford became known as Medicine Springs.[1] The mineral springs brought many famous visitors to the town and the streams furnished an abundance of power for the manufacturing plants. Fine woolen cassimeres and merino cloth were among Stafford's better-known products, but heavyweight meltons and kerseys were also produced. Hotels were built in this newly found resort area and the town prospered with the influx of "out of towners." Sulky racing became an exhilarating form of entertainment.

The community's fame as a medicinal spa was already well established when Myra Clark Lord was born on April 13, 1835. Her parents were John and Sally Spellman Lord. John Lord was a prominent contractor and builder of several mills, school-houses, and the old Congregational Church in Stafford. Myra attended local schools, and two months after her nineteenth birthday married Julius Converse. After finishing his schooling, Julius entered his father's business, the Mineral Springs Manufacturing Company, and as the years passed, rose step-by-step until he became the company's treasurer. In 1866, he assumed the title of Agent.

Coming from an established, well-known family, Myra was an active and respected woman in her own right, but her marriage to Julius made her the wife of one of the most influential men in town. The Converse residence, Woodlawn, was surrounded with spacious landscaped grounds and the house was known as one of the most beautiful and picturesque places in Connecticut. Myra and Julius had eight children, and along with their family and many social commitments, the house was a busy place. Myra participated in various women's organizations, and was a member of the First United Methodist Church of Stafford Springs. The symbols she included on her quilt and her membership in the church suggest Myra may also have been a member of the Degree of Rebekah, a women's organization affiliated with the Odd Fellows.

Julius died on June 7, 1892, after nearly thirty-nine years of marriage. Myra continued to live a full life until her death in 1912.

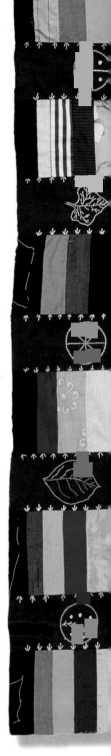

Photo of Woodlawn.
Courtesy of Stafford Historical Society, Inc., Stafford Springs, Connecticut.

Chinese Coins, 1897, made by Myra Lord Converse, Stafford Springs, silk, 47" x 56". Owned by
Cynthia Warren Mahdalik. The quilt was a gift to Myra's granddaughter, Eugenia Converse Lee,
on her fifteenth birthday in 1897. It is signed and dated *"Eugenia C. Lee from M.L.C. 1897."*

Claribel Emogene Burlingame Carr

Claribel Emogene Burlingame was born on July 27, 1882 to Margaret Sever Baker Burlingame and Stephen Sweet Burlingame, Jr., in the village of Oneco in the town of Sterling. One of ten children, Claribel learned to sew from her mother and when her mother became handicapped, they made many quilts together. The original quilting frame still remains in the family.

Claribel's Friendship Crazy quilt was completed in February of 1899, shortly before her marriage. The quilt was constructed of woolen scraps cut and pieced like a traditional Crazy quilt. It contains Claribel's initials *"C.E.B."* as well as the initials of friends and relatives: *"F.L.D."* for Flora Dawley, *"J.M.M."* for Julia Mowry, *"B.M.K."* for Bertha Kenyan, and *"B.M.B."* for Bertha Burlingame, Claribel's sister. The embroidered initials and decorative featherstitching were done with multi-colored yarns.

Claribel married H. Levi Carr, a millwright, and the couple moved to the large industrial center of Manchester. The census records of 1915 show the family living on Summit Street along with their only child, four-year-old Thelma. The portrait of Claribel was probably taken around that time. It shows an attractive and thoughtful large-eyed woman, with her hair in a fashionable, yet conservative style. During the early years of her marriage, Claribel followed the traditional path of a homemaker. She was a member of the Methodist Church and participated in several of their activities, as well as in other voluntary organizations.

When World War I began, Claribel, like many other Connecticut women, assisted the local Red Cross Chapter by sewing necessary articles to be shipped overseas to military personnel and civilians in need. She joined in Red Cross activities again when World War II broke out. Levi died some time before the beginning of World War II, and Claribel entered the paying work force to support herself. She worked at the Cheney Brothers Mill making parachutes for the war effort. After the war, Claribel was employed by Mary Cheney Library for a number of years. She was ninety-seven years old when she died in Manchester on November 19, 1979.

Clara Emogene Burlingame Carr

Crazy Quilt, 1899, made by Claribel Emogene Burlingame Carr (1882-1979), Oneco, wool, 72" x 82". Owned by Thelma Carr Woodbridge.

Cornelia Ball Jenks

This jewel-toned, Log Cabin silk quilt with a velvet border was made by Cornelia Ball Jenks of Torrington, wife of George Jenks. Cornelia was born October 29, 1851 in Salisbury and was a life-long Connecticut resident.

This quilt was presented as a wedding gift to her nephew, Charles Edwin Clinton, upon his marriage to Marcia E. Hill at Torrington's First Congregational Church on October 31, 1901. Coincidentally, Charles is listed in the city directory at the time of his marriage as "an inspector of needles" for the Excelsior Needle Company, a premiere manufacturer of sewing needles. In 1898, the Excelsior Needle Company became an operating arm of the Torrington Company, producing needles for Connecticut sewing machine manufacturer Wheeler & Wilson, which went on to become a world leader in the manufacturer of bearings.

This quilt was clearly treasured and it was eventually donated to The Torrington Historical Society in lovely condition. Cornelia died in West Haven in 1918 from "chronic Bright's disease," and is buried in Torrington.

Promotional giveaway from The Torrington Company. "Twill hold any style or make of Needles—but good Torrington Needles are most at home inside it."

Log Cabin, 1901, made by Cornelia Ball Jenks (1851-1918), Torrington, silk and velvet, 59.5" x 67". Owned by The Torrington Historical Society.

126

Charles H. Riley

Charles Riley is given the credit for making these quilts, precisely sewn with strong, dark, masculine colors. All but one is a Log Cabin. As his descendant stated, "They reflect the artistic-engineering sense in his character." It is believed that it was Charles who signed only one of his quilts in blocked, straight, draftsman-like letters.

It is hard to conceive that a blacksmith would have the inclination to make such remarkable quilts. His family remembers that he did not receive a formal education. He spent much of his time drafting mechanical devices that he could have received patents for. Sometime in the middle years of his life, Charles, an Irishman born in Norwalk in 1855, developed a fascination for Log Cabin quilts. Besides the quilts, his family also has the drawings of his inventions. It was not until 1906 that he finally married. Mary Gorman was just sixteen years of age when she and Charles wed.

Charles and Mary lived in a small house in Southport Center, a section of Fairfield, close to where his smithy was located. They had one child, a daughter named Maude. His grandsons do not remember observing their grandfather's needle skills as these quilts would have been made long before their birth; however, the Riley grandchildren remember their grandmother and do not recollect her ever sewing. Charles died at the age of seventy-three in 1928. Mary survived her husband by thirty-three years and died in 1961.

Puss in the Corner, c. 1890-1925, made by Charles H. Riley, Southport Center, cotton, 67.5" x 77". Owned by members of the Seirup Family.

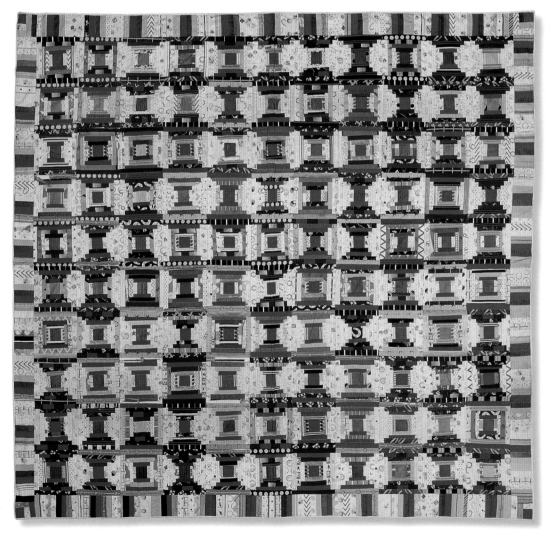

Courthouse Steps, c. 1890-1925, made by Charles H. Riley, Southport Center, cotton, 84.5" x 90.5". Owned by members of the Seirup Family.

Pineapple, c. 1890-1925, made by Charles H. Riley, Southport Center, cotton, 80" x 69". Owned by members of the Seirup Family.

Courthouse Steps, c. 1875-1910, made by Charles H. Riley, Southport Center, satin and silk, 62" x 70". Owned by members of the Seirup Family.

129

Angie Estelle Goodwin

When Harriett Curtis Bissell left her quilts to her granddaughter, Angie, she gave her a sampler of patterns and a legacy of quiltmaking. Angie, however, influenced by the surroundings of another era, chose the popular Dresden Plate pattern—adding a floral twist for style—when designing a quilt for a special niece, Myrtle.[1]

Angie, one of ten children born to Hubbard Leonard Goodwin and Harriet Sophia Bissell Goodwin, grew up on the family farm in Torrington, part of the fourth generation to farm the property purchased by Hubbard's great-grandfather, Isaac Goodwin, in 1761. Angie never married, but left the family home to live in Winsted, spending her time in service to others. Myrtle's parents kept a bedroom for her at their home in Torrington and when Angie had a quilt top ready for quilting, she would travel to her brother's house by bus. When they saw her coming up the street they would get out the quilt frame and set it up in the living room. Mrs. Johnson, a neighbor and good friend of Angie's, would come over and join in the quilting. The two ladies were serious quilters and did not like to be disturbed. Angie would stay for as long as it took to finish the quilt and then return home to continue her work, returning periodically for holidays, birthdays, or to quilt another quilt. Oddly, she never taught her niece, Myrtle to quilt but she did teach her other forms of needlework. Myrtle is a quiltmaker today, however, developing the seed planted in her by Aunt Angie.

Angie Estelle Goodwin

Dresden Plate, c. 1925-1950, made by Angie Estelle Goodwin (1868-1946), Winsted, cotton, 92" x 85". Owned by Myrtle Goodwin Dobos.

Stella Jewett Godard

Stella Jewett was born on January 28, 1872 to Granby natives, Frederick Jenner Jewett and Mary Cooley Jewett, while they were living in Cleveland, Ohio. On March 27, 1894, at the age of twenty-two, Stella married Oliver C. Godard, a Granby farmer.[1] Following in the family's musical tradition, Stella was an organist at the First Congregational Church in Granby and the originator of Music Sunday, an annual tradition at church to this day.

Redwork became the embroidery/quilting rage of the last quarter of the nineteenth century. Contrary to the Crazy quilt embroidery theme, in which nearly every seam and open space was adorned with the fancywork of its maker, redwork was crisp and appealing, with open spaces of usually white cotton fabric. The motifs chosen by each maker usually illustrated the favorite things of her life. At least one company in the state, the Connecticut Manufacturing Company, was selling perforated patterns for redwork designs as shown in *Harper's Bazaar*, January 30, 1887.[2] Perhaps the best clues to Stella's inspiration for making this quilt can be found on the quilt itself. The obvious courting scene and the open-hearth motif most certainly suggest this was made in anticipation of her marriage to Ollie in 1894.

Stella Jewett Godard entered her thirty-six block, summer redwork quilt in the Granby Grange Agricultural Fair in the early 1920s. It was awarded a first prize of fifty cents.[3] Her redwork motifs are representative of the 1890 to 1925 era of redwork quilts, but it is the decorative embroidery of the floral sashing that makes this quilt truly special.

Stella lived the last years of her life in Florida. She died in 1948 and is buried in the Granby Center Cemetery.[4]

This courting scene may have been included in anticipation of Stella's marriage in 1894.

Redwork Quilt, c. 1890-1925, made by Stella Jewett Godard (1872-1948), Granby, cotton, 71" x 77". Owned by Salmon Brook Historical Society.

Under the Red Cross Flag

*I*t was May 10, 1917, just one month after a State of War was declared with Germany. President Wilson announced the formation of a War Council to financially aid the War effort. His request was simply this, "To raise great sums of money for the support of the work to be done…upon a great scale." The response of the citizens of the United States was one of the greatest benevolent achievements accomplished on a national scale.[1]

The American Red Cross was founded on May 21, 1881 by Miss Clara Barton, a Civil War nurse. This organization disregarded the boundaries of religion, creed, nationality, race, and sex. Throughout the following fifty years, the Red Cross assumed relief efforts for famine, floods, epidemics, earthquakes, and other natural disasters both in the United States and overseas. Its first local chapter was begun in Danville, New York in 1881 at the Lutheran Church. In June 1900, the American National Red Cross was incorporated by an Act of Congress.[2]

Throughout World War I, the Red Cross increased in size from 562 chapters with 500,000 members to 3,724 chapters, 17,000 branches, and over thirty-one million members, including adults and children. In the Hartford area alone, the fifty Auxiliaries in the summer of 1917 increased to 160 Auxiliaries and twenty-one branches by the time the armistice came. They were sending out a weekly quota of four thousand to five thousand items and the same number of gifts. At first, production was done by individuals who took these items home. When the demand began to rise, sewing circles assumed responsibility and opened Red Cross workrooms in community churches:

> *Women came and went at all hours, giving all of their time that was theirs to give. It was a task that was nobly executed because of the determined energy and unselfish devotion of the many workers.*[3]

The December 1917 issue of *Modern Priscilla* included a precise pattern, design, and instructions for a quilt that was in keeping with the absolute rules of the Red Cross. Quilters were encouraged to make the quilt to raise funds for the War effort. Detailed instructions provided 536 spaces to write the names of contributors and a specific cash amount was recommended for each space. The larger spaces were more costly. If this fundraiser was planned and conducted according to the instructions, $1,009 could be raised. The original quilt instructions were planned by Clara Washburn Angell.[4]

The challenge was accepted nationwide. State documentation teams in New York, Ohio, New Jersey, and Arizona documented quilts made for Red Cross fundraising. In Hartford, the Ladies Aid Society of the Windsor Avenue Congregational Church accepted the challenge to make this quilt. Their successful effort raised $1,150, exceeding even the recommended amount in *Modern Priscilla.* The quilt design is nearly identical to the original instructions. A center medallion with a larger diamond white area is the only alteration of the original instructions. Signed on the quilt were the names of the men and women from their church serving in the War with their addresses and branches of the military. It is a lasting memorial recognizing those who served both on the home front and in Europe.

Dramatic pose of Red Cross worker demonstrating her patriotic spirit during World War I. *Photo courtesy of John Woodall.*

Red Cross, c. 1918, made by The Ladies' Aid Society of the Windsor Avenue Congregational Church, Hartford, cotton, 83" x 94". *Courtesy of The Connecticut Historical Society. Acc#A.1622. Photo by David Stansbury.*

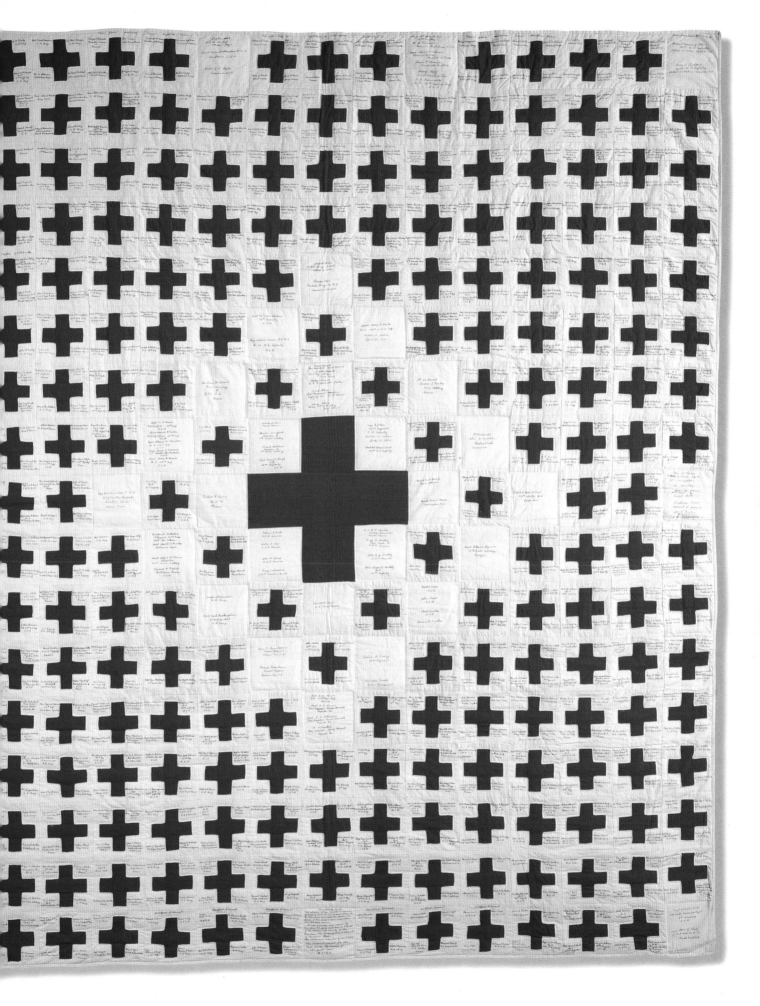

133

Lenora Whitney Walbridge

*L*enora Whitney grew up in the town of Stafford Springs. This northeastern Connecticut town had long developed a reputation for its iron ore fields, the production of stoves, and its textile mills. In the late eighteenth century, mineral springs in the area triggered its rebirth as a spa town. Lenora married Will Walbridge, a Stafford Springs' shop owner. They raised four children: two boys and two girls. Before retirement in 1930, Will and Lenora moved to Old Mystic. They were life-long members of the Methodist Church. Lenora died at the age of seventy-six and is buried in the Elm Grove Cemetery in Mystic.

The red, green, and white fabric of Lenora's pineapple appliqué quilt is from the 1920s. It was a ribbon winner at two agricultural fairs: a Special Premium at the Stafford Springs Agricultural Fair, and at the North Stonington Grange Fair in 1930. The county agricultural, grange, and church fairs have long been considered a New England institution and were usually the social highlight of the year. These annual events provided the stage for Connecticut's rural residents to showcase their crops, livestock, preserves, handwork, and needlework. Awards and ribbons such as Lenora's were eagerly sought after and proudly displayed along with the prize-winning quilts.

Pineapple Appliqué, c. 1920, made by Lenora Whitney Walbridge (1868-1944), Stafford, cotton, 79" x 98". Privately owned.

Edith Grace Buck Bidwell

*T*he life of Edith Grace Buck Bidwell spanned most of the twentieth century. She lived to the grand age of ninety and had a very full life. Edith was born September 3, 1907 in Hebron, the daughter of Clinton E. and Grace Weir Buck. She was of English ancestry and a true Yankee.

In the early 1920s, Edith began working at the Cheney Brothers Mills in Manchester as an inspector of the silk cloth used to make neckties. Her enjoyment of fabric began at an early age with her One-Patch tied comfortable made in 1925 using samples of this necktie fabric. This quilt contains 575 pieces approximately three inches square. The backing is floral-printed cotton.

Cheney Brothers was an industrial empire, at one time the largest silk complex in the world. It covered more than thirty-six acres of land and employed over five thousand men and women of all nationalities. Life as a young adult in a factory town such as Manchester, however, did not mean all work. The Cheney family provided factory housing and a library for their employees. They hosted social events consisting of lectures, concerts, and dances at Cheney Hall. In return, the Cheneys expected full cooperation from their work force with long, physically demanding hours.

Edith married Ray W. Bidwell and had one daughter and two sons. They made their home in Manchester while Ray worked for Pratt & Whitney Aircraft. Edith was a member of the South United Methodist Church and participated in many church functions. As the Bidwell family grew, and as her daily home and community obligations increased, quilting gradually moved into the background of Edith's life.

During World War II, like many other Connecticut women, Edith returned to the work force as an inspector of cloth at the Addison Velvet Mills in Glastonbury. At the age of thirty-eight, she resumed her quilting activities by making a tied scrap quilt of multi-colored velvets. Her daughter is the current owner of these two quilts and continues to live in the family home.

Advertisement for Cheney Brothers silk.

Bricks, c. 1925, made by Edith Grace Buck Bidwell (1907-1998), Manchester, silk, 79" x 82". Owned by Grace Bidwell Longo.

Edith Grace Buck Bidwell

One-Patch, c. 1945, made by Edith Grace Buck Bidwell (1907-1998), Manchester, silk, 79" x 82". Owned by Grace Bidwell Longo.

Lucy Leete

The town of Guilford's name was Menunkatuck in 1639 when Lucy Leete's ancestors first arrived in Connecticut with Henry Whitfield. The planters, as they were called, were allotted a portion of land in the new wilderness.

> *The first planters who came to the town were of two ranks, viz, such as who in England are called gentlemen and commonality. None were poor men, and few or no servants…The gentlemen were all men of wealth, and they bear the appellation of Mr…while according to the plain customs of those times the commonality were named only Goodman or Neighbor.*[1]

Lucy's ancestors lived at the corner of Petticoat Lane and York Street. This section of Guilford was called Leete Lane.[2] Agriculture was the town's principal business and there were only a few stores set up near the Green. The harbor at Sachem's Head, the section of Guilford on the Sound, was small and shallow with many rocks. The Great Ox Pasture overlooking Sachem's Head was a bluff owned by the Leete family. It was from this point that the Revolutionary War volunteers prevented the British from overtaking a number of whaling boats in the harbor and defending Guilford soil on June 17, 1777.[3] The Guilford troops were victorious in this skirmish.

A little over two hundred years later, the town of Guilford is still close to its roots. The oldest stone house in Connecticut and maybe New England is still a short distance from the Green. In the harbor at Sachem's Head, the British are long gone but the Great Ox Pasture once owned by the Leete family is still a pastoral scene. It is possible this is where Lucy Leete was inspired to chose these perky, bright, field flowers to embroider repeatedly on her quilt. The Sawtooth pattern is reminiscent of some of the earliest patterns that her quilting ancestors might have used. Although this quilt is signed *"ML 1927,"* its owner attributes the quilt to Lucy Leete.

Sawtooth, 1927, attributed to Lucy Leete, Guilford, cotton, 77" x 67". Owned by Theresa C. Kovacs.

Mary L. Burlingame Pirie

Mary L. Burlingame Pirie used postage stamp sized squares to construct her quilt. With an eye for the dramatic expression of color and beauty, she created a quilt resembling a modern, abstract painting. Around 1950, at the age of sixty-eight, Mary made her quilt with synthetic fabrics. To soften the geometric design, she appliquéd cutout flowers across the quilt and quilted the layers in a simple design with yellow thread five stitches to the inch.

Mary Burlingame's mother was from Pawtucket, Rhode Island, the birth place of the first cotton mill. Her father came from Crompton, another Rhode Island textile-mill village. Mary was born in Providence, Rhode Island, on June 28, 1872 to Margaret Sever Baker Burlingame and Stephen Sweet Burlingame, Jr. Shortly after Mary's birth, the family relocated to Oneco, a textile-mill village in Sterling, Connecticut.

Mary married George Pirie, a stone cutter and quarryman, in 1890 and moved to Manchester. All the major relocations in her life followed the textile trail, from the mill towns of Rhode Island to those of the textile-producing centers of eastern Connecticut. George and Mary had eight children: three sons and five daughters. The quiltmaker's great-granddaughter currently owns this quilt. She remembers her great-grandmother for her love of gardening, flower arranging, baking, cake decorating, sewing, and her prolific quiltmaking. This quilt was entered in an exhibit sponsored by the Knights of Pythias Grange where it won a blue ribbon.

Mary L. Burlingame Pirie

138

Postage Stamp, c. 1925-1950, made by
Mary L. Burlingame Pirie, Manchester,
cotton, 69" x 86". Owned by Heather
Schaefer Crowne.

Minnie Pearl Pardee Barrett's Roosevelt Rose

Minnie Pearl Pardee Barrett is remembered by her family as a woman who was passionate about everything she did. When her favorite political figure, Franklin D. Roosevelt, was elected the thirty-second President of the United States in 1933, she honored him and his wife, Eleanor, by making this appliqué, floral Medallion quilt. Using a pattern designed by Republican Ruth Finley, who presented the identical quilt to the First Lady, Minnie created her own version in 1935.[1] Minnie also hooked a rug, which is now at the Little White House, FDR's home in White Springs, Georgia.

Minnie Pearl Pardee was born in Ridgefield on June 15, 1874. After she completed eighth grade in the local school, she moved to the more industrial town of Bristol. Minnie found work in Woolworth's Five and Ten Cents Store. At the age of nineteen, she married William L. Barrett, from Pine Plains, New York. William opened and operated a successful glass-cutting business and was the sole support of their family of five children.

Minnie's granddaughters remember that their grandmother "was not active in politics, and as a matter of fact had to be very obedient to her husband." Her loyalty to President Roosevelt, however, was legendary. Her granddaughters recalled that each time Roosevelt won an election, Minnie took a big cowbell and went outside to ring it at midnight. Minnie responded to his call for civilian support during World War II by knitting socks, mittens, and scarves for the soldiers on the front lines. They also remember Sunday family dinners when their other grandmother was present. This grandmother was as ardent a Republican as Minnie was a Democrat. At times the children feared the mashed potatoes would start flying because of the intensity of the political debate between the two grandmothers.

It was with great pride that Minnie entered her treasured quilt into Danbury State Fair in the late 1930s and was awarded a blue ribbon. Minnie died in 1958 at the age of eighty-four.

Minnie Pearl Pardee Barrett

The Roosevelt Rose, c. 1935, made by Minnie Pearl Pardee Barrett (1874-1958), Bristol, cotton, 90" x 101". Owned by Holly J. Barrett.

Gladys Hall Melius

*T*he old adage "if you want a job done, give it to a busy person" certainly applied to quilter Gladys Hall Melius. Born the daughter of Chauncey and Emily Curtiss Hart Hall, she was one of eleven children and grew up in the Terryville/Harwinton area. She married Frank Melius and although they only had one child, a son Franklin, her life was always full of activities.

Besides helping her husband operate the family gas station in Terryville, she was renown locally for the gladiolus and strawberries she raised and sold from a roadside stand for many years. The memories her nieces and nephews hold dearest are those of the wonderful popcorn balls she made from seeds she had planted in the spring and gave to each of the children for Christmas every year. Between the planting, growing, selling, and cooking, however, Gladys still managed to produce a veritable crop of delightful quilts.

Gladys's twin quilts are a variation of the Barbara Frietchie Star. According to a 1931 article in *Needle Craft Magazine*,[1] Barbara Frietchie is credited with a quilt found in her home that presented an eight-point star pattern, reminiscent of the patriotism she was immortalized for in John Greenleaf Whittier's poem, "Barbara Frietchie." Whittier claims that the elderly Frietchie defied Confederate troops under Stonewall Jackson by waving the stars and stripes from her upstairs window as they advanced through Frederick, Maryland. When threatened with death for her actions, she supposedly shouted, "Shoot, if you must, this old gray head, but spare your country's flag." Jackson forbade his men to shoot her, and her flag flew triumphantly above their heads.

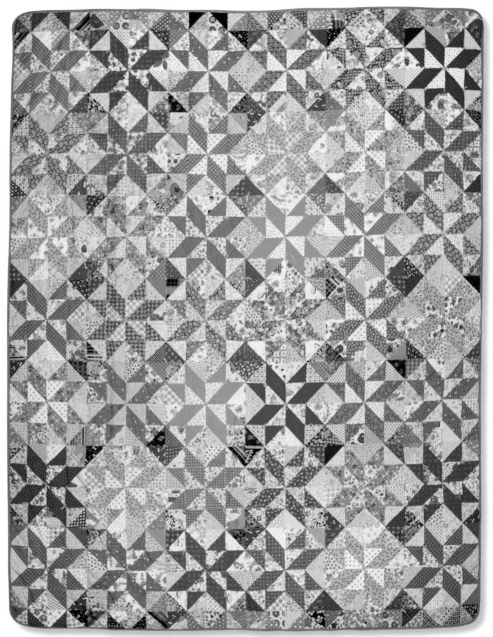

Barbara Frietchie Star Variation, c. 1925-1950, made by Gladys Hall Melius (1898-1993), Terryville, cotton, 69" x 86". Owned by Joyce R. Atwood. One of a pair of nearly identical quilts.

Gladys Hall Melius

141

Maie Mallette

This 1930s era daffodil appliqué quilt has a unique story demonstrating its maker's love for youth that has continued through two unrelated Connecticut families.

While airing a collection of quilts one day, the current owner's six-year old son pulled this one from the pile, laid his ear against it, and announced elatedly, "I can hear a heartbeat in this quilt!" Struck by his absolute conviction, the owner, in remembering the quilt's past, was not surprised. "Well, when you make something for someone you love, it's hard to keep the heartbeat out of it," she responded. He nodded wisely, gave the quilt a pat, and went off to play convinced that particular quilt lived on. And in a way it does.

Made by Maie Mallette, a lifelong Torrington resident, for a dearly loved niece some sixty years earlier, its gift of love has sustained. Maie was born on New Year's Eve, 1894, the daughter of Eugene Mallette and Eva Fowler Mallette. According to surviving family members, she was a meticulous, refined woman who was the master of any needlework she set her hand to. A skilled and respected dressmaker, she frequently worked for Litchfield County's wealthy clientele. Although she never married, and lived with a bachelor brother after her parents passed away, she adored her young nieces and nephews. Remembered as "a real taskmaster" by the niece for whom this quilt was made, she was also recalled as an adoring and generous aunt who encouraged her nieces to learn the ladies' handwork of the day. Regardless of the child's skill, she was quick to offer loving guidance, graciously encourage their projects, and delight in the time they shared together. Her expectations of excellence went beyond the sewing circle, for she also insisted that they abide by all the rules of etiquette, attend church regularly, and live an honorable and moral life.

Much of Maie's free time was devoted to her church, Torrington's Trinity Episcopal, where she was the director of religion for many years. Today, Maie's heartbeat lives on, not only in the memories of her own family, but in the family who now owns the quilt, and in the understanding of their son for whom the quilt carries a lesson about the power of love.

Daffodil Appliqué, c. 1930, made by Maie Mallette (1894-1976), Torrington, cotton, 74" x 88". Owned by M. E. Ford.

Maie Mallette

142

The Hired Man's Quilt

No quilt exemplifies New England practicality more vividly than this "hired man's quilt." Made by Annie McIlravey Emmons of the Lakeside section of Morris during the 1930s, it graphically recycles the everyday clothing of a working man into a quilt of contemporary fashion.

Annie McIlravey was born in Washington, Connecticut, a stone's throw from the town of Morris where she spent the quilting years of her life. Prior to marrying Dwight Emmons and her subsequent move to the farm that had been his father's, Annie had been a schoolteacher—a career two of her four daughters would also pursue. For the better part of the Emmons' life together, their families, children, and grandchildren gathered at the classic Connecticut farm for Thanksgiving.

Since the Emmons' farm was a large dairy farm on substantial acreage, the couple had a hired man for many years. Unlike other farms where the help often had separate housing, their hired man had his own accommodations within the large family farmhouse. "It was a big old farmhouse and the hired man just lived in a separate part of it," recalls their granddaughter, Mary, who owns the quilt today. She was not surprised at its construction. "They were very practical people, and she probably used what she had on hand," Mary said.

Unfortunately, Annie had gone blind from diabetes by the time Mary was twelve, and although they remained close, Mary regrets that they were never able to share a quilting experience. Her mother, however, does recall ladies gathering at the farm to piece quilts, and for Saturday night bridge games that Annie enjoyed. Although the farm has passed into the realm of history, the quilt remains a link to one of Connecticut's early dairy farms and the practical eye of one woman.

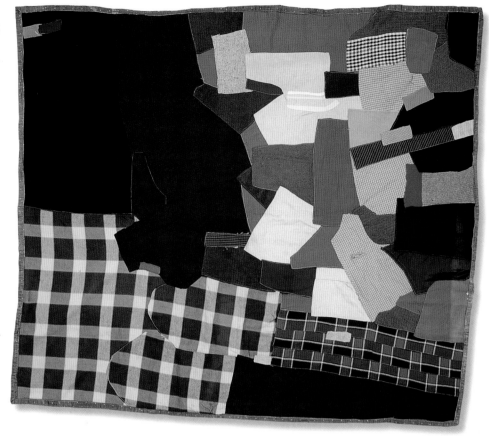

Scrap Quilt, c. 1930, made by Annie McIlravey Emmons (1886-1958), Morris, wool, 66" x 75". Owned by Mary W. Curtiss.

Feedsack fabric from the reverse of the quilt.

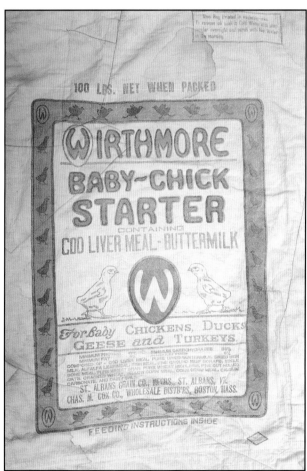

Annie McIlravey Emmons

143

Rose Adah Baldwin Dawe

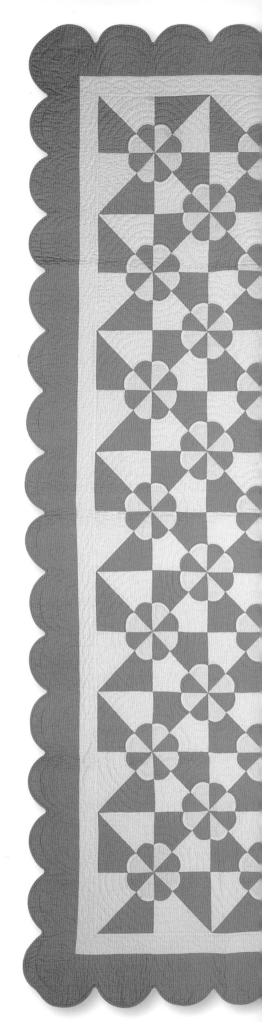

Rose Adah Baldwin was born on June 11, 1885 in Burlington. She was the daughter of Edward and Mary Patterson Baldwin. Edward was a farmer and Mary was a homemaker, and both were of English and "Scotch-Irish" ancestry. Rose attended school in Burlington and completed the eighth grade. She attended the Burlington Congregational Church and in 1911 she married John Grosvenor Dawe. Dawe was a farmer as Rose's father had been, and the couple lived in the Forestville section of Bristol. They had four children: Ruth, Marjorie, Edna, and John.

After her marriage, Rose worked at home as a dressmaker. She used many of her leftover scraps in making her numerous quilts, and daughter Edna remembers helping her mother. Rose loved gardening and grew many kinds of cacti. She also had a rock garden that she enjoyed working in when she was not quilting.

The family seemed to have adequate goods during the Depression, but it only happened because of good planning. According to daughter Edna, the lessons in frugality taught them to do the best they could with what they had and to be thrifty and not waste anything. It was during these years of hard work that Rose entered her quilt in a contest sponsored by the Bristol department store, Muzzy Brothers. She won the First Prize of $10 cash! Rose presented her prize-winning quilt to her daughter, Edna, and her new son-in-law, Charles Tuttle, as a wedding gift on May 15, 1937.

Rose died in 1973, and each time Edna sees the prizewinner she recalls those happy times when she sat with her mother making quilts.

Rose Adah Baldwin Dawe and her husband, John

144

Primrose Hearts and Gizzards, 1937,
made by Rose Adah Baldwin Dawe
(1885-1973), Bristol, cotton, 85" x 94".
Owned by Edna Tuttle.

Harriet Goldsmith Monroe Hopkins

arriet Goldsmith Monroe Hopkins was born in Hartford on January 9, 1879, the daughter of George Brother Monroe and Carrie Marie Swain Monroe. On May 31, 1899, she married William Henry Hopkins in Norwich, where they raised a family of two daughters and a son. It was not until her later years that Harriet took to quilting as a pastime, deciding to make quilts for each of her daughters and her only grandchild, Betty Ann.

Betty Ann's mother worked long hours as a private duty nurse, so Betty Ann spent a great deal of time with her grandmother, much to their mutual delight. Consequently, a pictorial crib quilt of the three little pigs was the first project tackled by Harriet. No stranger to the needle before she began quilting, Harriet made nearly all of Betty Ann's clothing, including undergarments to match the outfits. It was not until Betty Ann was in school that she realized not everyone had such ensembles!

Knowing that her health was declining due to diabetes, Harriet pressed her two daughters to choose a quilt pattern. The quilt pattern that one of her daughters eventually chose, the Hawaiian style appliqué, was intriguing. When this quilt was documented, the pattern was not typical of the era in which it was purported to have been made. In addition, examination of the quilt suggested that two different sets of hands had worked the stitching, which only added to the confusion. Had the quilt been started in the late 1800s and finished at a later date? Excellent records that accompanied the quilt dismissed that as a possibility, and further research provided the answers.

Betty Ann's mother was often assigned to private duty care along what was later known as Connecticut's "Gold Coast"—a group of wealthy communities harboring large, private homes. It was on one of these assignments, while caring for a Mrs. Rudy, wife of a prominent jeweler, that a quilt on her patient's bed caught her eye. According to Betty Ann, her mother traced the pattern of the lovely antique quilt and gave it to Harriet to reproduce. By the time Harriet began the project, however, her health had begun to decline significantly, so Betty Ann's mother assisted with the appliqué, leaving the finer quilting work to her mother.

Betty Ann recalls that each quilt took three to four years to make, with her grandmother working at the dining room table long after the dishes had been cleared away. Just prior to her passing away, Harriet completed her final quilt, which was promised to her other daughter. Now all three quilts remain with Betty Ann, along with the memories of a doting grandmother rising early in the morning to surprise her with fresh apple pie and a warm loaf of bread.

Harriet Goldsmith Monroe Hopkins with her daughter

Hawaiian Style Appliqué, c. 1925-1950, made by Harriet Goldsmith Monroe Hopkins (1879-1944), Norwich, cotton, 69" x 68". Owned by Betty Ann Apicelli Chapman.

Frances Lucy Guinchi Baldi

*N*ot all women were prolific quiltmakers. Some, like Frances Lucy Baldi, were inspired by a special pattern and made only one quilt.

In 1904, Frances' father, already an established shoemaker in Litchfield, returned to his homeland in Meldola, Italy, to bring his family to their new home in Connecticut. It was not unusual for the man of the family to immigrate to the United States and set up a home before sending for his family. On the way to the train station, Frances's father told the young boy who drove them, "If you give us a good ride, I'll let you marry my daughter."

Arriving in Litchfield, they settled into the life he prepared for them but it was not long before their life changed. Frances's father was killed in a tragic buggy accident near their home, and she had to quit school to help the family. She had only reached the eighth grade. At the age of seventeen happenstance reunited her with the boy from the train station, Michael Antonio Baldi, and they married. Tony worked for a local farmer and Frances cooked for the farmhands. Together they had two children, Albert and Edith, but Albert did not survive World War II. Edith married Wilbur Coffill in 1948 and they gave Frances two grandsons and a granddaughter. In 1960, when her husband died, Frances became a self-employed seamstress. Not only did she work until she was ninety, but she was very active in her church as well as in the Morgan-Weir Post #27 American Legion Auxiliary. She continued to sew as well as knit and crochet throughout her life. Frances taught her grand-daughter how to sew at a young age, sitting her on her lap while she worked the treadle of her old Singer.

In the 1940s, Frances purchased a quilt kit from a local department store.[1] She skillfully finished the appliqué pattern stamped on the background fabric, but did not complete the quilting pattern formed by consecutive dots. When the top was completed, she displayed it on the bed in her sewing room where she could enjoy it while she worked. In the early 1980s, it was hand quilted by a lady from Washington, Connecticut, a gift from her grandson.

Frances Lucy Guinchi Baldi

Flowers, c. 1945, made by Francis Lucy Guinchi Baldi (1895-1993), Litchfield, cotton, 77" x 93". Owned by Roberta M. Coffill.

Sarah Eva Watrous Pomeroy

Known as a naturalist, lecturer, teacher, and librarian superintendent, Sarah Eva Watrous Pomeroy was one of those women who did everything well. She was born in Meriden on September 19, 1883 to John and Rosa Watrous. One of Sarah's ancestors was William Brewster, the leader of the Puritans who founded Plymouth Colony. Her father, a forward thinking man, cultivated and marketed the first peaches in the area. Sarah's mother bore thirteen children and assisted her husband in managing their large holdings and the many farmhands needed to keep their orchards profitable. Her family's commitment to the land most certainly influenced Sarah's passion for nature and the great outdoors.

At the age of sixteen, Sarah was enrolled in the New Haven Normal School, founded for the training of Connecticut teachers. By the time she was twenty, she had been appointed the teaching principal of a small rural school in Killingworth. Later, she took further education classes at Yale University and earned lifetime teaching certificates for both Connecticut and New Jersey. She and Howard Daniel Pomeroy, whose English ancestor was one of the first settlers of Windsor, were married on March 17, 1917 at her family's home.

Sarah and Howard moved to Florida shortly thereafter. Always a career woman, she continued her work as a naturalist and lecturer, and for a while was the librarian superintendent of thirteen counties in Florida. She and Howard lived full lives in the St. Petersburg area, and are now both buried in the Norfolk Center Cemetery in Norfolk, Connecticut.

For this Pinwheel quilt, Sarah used backing material that was woven cotton from the late 1930s, originally intended for covering the wings and fuselage of airplanes.[1] She had obtained the fabric from her son-in-law, Harold Fields. She may have chosen the pinwheel pattern to mimic the propellers of an airplane. The quilt won first place at an exhibit at Norfolk Town Hall in 1950.

Sarah Eva Watrous Pomeroy, c. 1903

Sarah's childhood home, Christian Hill, in Higganum. This handsome old Victorian is no longer standing, having unfortunately been taken down in the 1930s. In the wing on the right was the library where Sarah had happy memories of three-story tall Christmas trees.

Pinwheel Variation, 1949, made by Sarah Eva Watrous Pomeroy (1883-
1969), Middletown, cotton, 95.5" x 109". Owned by the Fields Family.

Gathered Together:
Philosophies of Connecticut Collectors

*by Carla Bue, Marilyn Cocking,
and Sue Reich*

The reasons for collecting quilts are as varied as the collections themselves. Art museums value quilts for their aesthetic qualities, as examples of folk art. Historical societies acquire quilts because they preserve many aspects of the local heritage, amounting almost to historical documents. Some individuals make and keep their own quilts, while others are attracted to a specific pattern, color, or time period. Quilt collections are treasures of our past and records of our present. The beauty they preserve would be enough in itself, but there is so much more.

Large institutions, such as the Connecticut Historical Society (CHS), are dedicated to the collection and preservation of Connecticut's history, heritage, artifacts, and documents, and to making this knowledge available to the public. Most of the quilts in the CHS collection came from Connecticut families who used them in everyday life, and they show a valuable cross section of periods and styles.

Smaller history museums and town historical societies display quilts naturally as part of household furnishings. Their collections include local artifacts representing inhabitants and events of a previous era. The Guilford's Hyland House is decorated in the style of a specific time in history to give a better understanding of what it really was like to live in "those days." People who present gifts to historical societies and museums share their ancestral treasures, yet at the same time they help to preserve the larger history of a town, state, and country.

Every collector uses his or her own individual justifications for adding to or eliminating pieces from the collection. A quilt may be valued as a beautiful object or for its varied combinations of fabrics and patterns. Those who inherit the family quilts may find memories of a beloved grandmother brought to mind by fabrics or pattern or a combination of colors. A quilt shop owner or antique dealer's collections are motivated by economic factors, eye appeal and resale value that at times may be more important than historical interest and provenance. Few private collectors have given serious consideration to what will happen to their quilts in the distant future. They are busy enjoying the collecting and refining process in the present. Perhaps they have the right approach. For a dispersed collection is not lost, it is only waiting for the next quilt lover to accept the challenge and joy of collecting.

Connecticut CQSP member Wanda Stolarun Dabrowski researched the existence of many Connecticut quilts in museum collections throughout the country. Her research documented Connecticut quilts in The Winterthur Museum, The Museum of Fine Arts Boston, Sturbridge Village, The Henry Ford Museum & Greenfield Village, The Metropolitan Museum of Art, The Newark Museum, The Shelburne Museum, The National Museum of American History; Smithsonian Institution, and The Art Institute of Chicago to name just a few.[1]

The Connecticut Quilt Search Project documented the collections of approximately thirty historical societies and museums, and quilts from some of these collections are featured throughout the book. The quilts and their owners showcased here, however, have been chosen to illustrate the entrepreneurial collector, the private collector, and three Connecticut families who have amassed amazing collections through generations of quiltmakers.

Entrepreneurial Collectors

Zelma Richmond Anderson

Judy Shea and Nancy Burns began their fabric business in the shoreline town of Clinton in 1979. The time was just after the nation's Bicentennial celebration and a quilting revival had taken hold. The business flourished until 1999 when it closed its doors to be replaced by Judy's online pattern and kit business named Harbor View Quilt Designs. Inspired by the colors, construction, and design of old quilts, Judy Shea has created over one hundred of her own quilts. Over the years she also has amassed a collection of over forty old quilts purchased at sales, antique shops, and from private owners. While Judy and Nancy were in business on Route 1 in Clinton, quilt owners eager to sell their family heirlooms often approached them. Occasionally, as in the case of Zelma Anderson's Girls quilt, Judy received the quilt as a gift.

Zelma was born in 1920, the only child of Ella and Mark Richmond. Zelma was a bright and creative child who graduated from high school the day after her fifteenth birthday. Her mother had encouraged her daughter to attend the Rhode Island School of Design; however, her practical thinking father insisted that she go to secretarial school. Obeying her father's wishes, she became a secretary until she married Charles Anderson. The couple settled in Old Saybrook with their only child, June.

In 1935, when Zelma was just fifteen years old, her mother had given her some colored pencils and sixty-three white squares of fabric. Recognizing Zelma's artistic ability, she challenged her daughter to draw on the blocks which were to be used in a quilt. The result was a collection of smiling, pensive, reflective, and musing faces of women with outfits, hairdos, and makeup of the 1930s. Zelma never liked the quilt top that her mother constructed from the hand-colored blocks.

Over the years, Zelma has enjoyed all forms of needlework, and has used her gifts of design and creativity to make over fifty quilts. Her life is filled with activities and friends, which may be the secret of her longevity. On one of her regular visits to her favorite fabric store, J&N Fabrics in Clinton, she presented the quilt to one of the store's owners, Judy Shea, and this happy 1930s quilt has been the link of their good friendship throughout all these years.

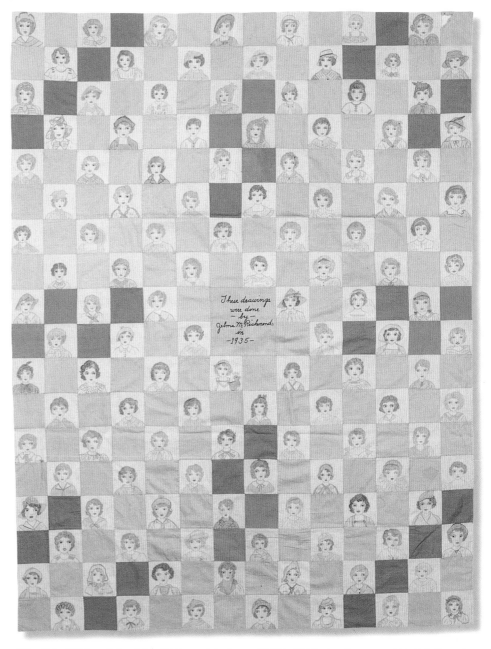

The Girls, 1935, made by Zelma Richmond Anderson (1920-), Old Saybrook, cotton, 84" x 89". Owned by Judy Shea.

Family Collections

Bertha Havens Thompson Peck

Bertha Havens Thompson was born in 1861, at the beginning of the Civil War, to Charles Augustus Thompson and Grace Antoinette Manville in East Haven. She lived her entire life in the New Haven area. In 1889, she married Newton J. Peck of Woodbridge. Together, they raised three children in the Peck family home on Ansonia Road. A housewife and mother first, Bertha always found time to become involved in community projects and her church.

Bertha is remembered for her love of sewing. Family memoirs record that she matched the plaids on every seam. Her quilts, in popular turn-of-the-century patterns, reflect her thriftiness in saving every scrap. A prolific quilter, her sewing fabric remnants were made into now treasured family heirlooms.

Bertha Havens Thompson Peck

Chips & Whetstones, c. 1890-1925, made by Bertha Havens Thompson Peck (1861-1936), Woodbridge, cotton, 79" x 98". Owned by Susan P. Bacon.

Nine-Patch, c. 1865-1890, made by Bertha Havens Thompson Peck (1861-1936), Woodbridge, cotton, 87" x 94". Owned by Polly P. Schulz.

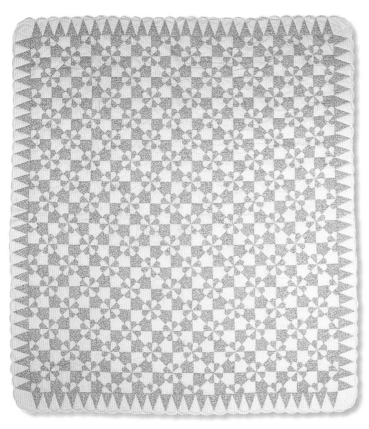

Hearts and Gizzards, c. 1925-1950, made by Bertha Havens Thompson Peck (1861-1936), Woodbridge, cotton, 78" x 87". Owned by Polly P. Schulz.

Delectable Mountains, c. 1865-1890, made by Bertha Havens Thompson Peck (1861-1936), Woodbridge, cotton, 76" x 75". Owned by Susan P. Bacon.

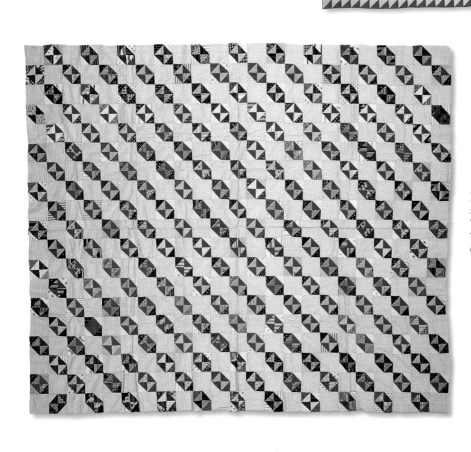

Broken Dishes, c. 1890-1925, made by Bertha Havens Thompson Peck (1861-1936), Woodbridge, cotton, 74" x 89". Owned by Susan P. Bacon.

The Haviland/Akin Descendants' Quilt Collection

How often have you heard someone wish they had inherited a family collection of photographs, the old farmhouse furniture, or the family coverlets and quilts? Can you imagine being the recipient of *all* of the above? The generations and time seem to have often determined by default that Lenora Buck would end up as the caretaker of much of her family's ancestral possessions. She has been the repository for outstanding collections of family quilts, coverlets, and furniture. Living her life surrounded by the domestic possessions of her ancestors and keeping their history is a charge that she has taken most seriously.

Lenora's nineteenth-century quilts have been passed down through four generations. The quilters were the daughters, daughters by marriage, and granddaughters of Abby Jane Ferriss Haviland. Abby Jane and her sister, Arabella Ferriss Marsh, were the quiltmakers of the Zachariah Ferriss quilt from New Milford.

Lenora's mother was Edith Florence Akin Vincent, her grandmother was Nettie Elizabeth Haviland Akin, and her great-grandparents were Florence Elizabeth Briggs Haviland and Tudor Haviland. Tudor Haviland, whose name is on the Zachariah Ferriss quilt, was the son of Abby Jane Ferriss Haviland and the grandson of Hannah and Zachariah Ferriss.

Lenora is committed to keeping and identifying the old family photos and their homesteads, documenting their travels back and forth across the state line from New Milford and Sherman to its western neighboring town of Patterson, New York. Her continual quest of researching family documents will provide her children and grandchildren with a true ancestral treasure.

Sunflower, c. 1840-1865, made by Gertrude A. Tipple, cotton, 75" x 94". Owned by Haviland/Akin descendants.

Sunburst, c. 1865-1890, made by Florence Briggs Haviland, cotton, 74" x 83". Owned by Haviland/Akin descendants.

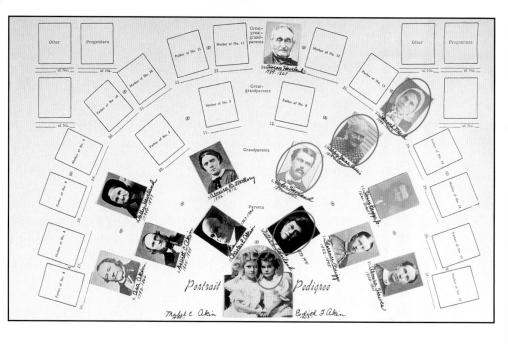

Family Tree showing how the quilts were passed down through Lenora Buck's family.

156

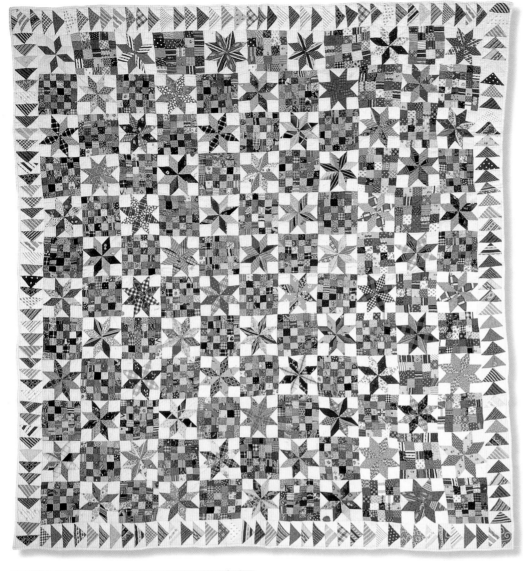

LeMoyne Star, c. 1840-1865, made by Florence Briggs Haviland, cotton, 74.5" x 79". Owned by Haviland/Akin descendants.

Florence Briggs Haviland

Lenora Buck

Feathered Star, c. 1840-1865, made by Haviland/Akin Descendants, cotton, 73" x 90". Owned by Haviland/Akin Descendants.

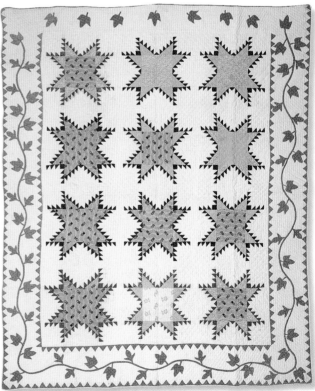

A Family Legacy

by Carla Bue

Collecting is sometimes inherited, whether we are aware of it or not. My first experience at age ten occurred when my grandparents, Anna and Harvy Godard, inherited over one hundred old bed quilts from Aunt Lavinna Wilson's estate when she died at age ninety-nine in the late 1950s. This collection created quite a stir in the family. With prolific quiltmakers on all sides, I not only received this collection from my grandparents, but over the years I acquired others because I expressed concern and interest in the preservation of the family's quilting heritage. My family also knew I would cherish them.

These first quilts descended from the family of my maternal grandfather, Harvey Godard. The surnames include Godard, Case, White, Beach, and Root. Family-made from 1840 to 1900 in Canton and North Granby, these quilts involved many helping hands and skill levels. A farm family and makers of cider brandy, the Godard "men folk" were graduates of Yale University—quite an accomplishment for the times. Interestingly, while the ladies had the means to buy printed fabric for the backs of their quilts, they chose cheaper cotton muslin rather than the more expensive printed fabric common in other quilts from the collection. The quilts display very fine quilting stitches and lovely, colorful pieced patterns. A special quilt in the collection is a sentimental signature quilt with many family names: Uncle Porter, Aunt Sophia, etc. Many are signed, initialed, numbered and dated. A Crazy quilt actually has the Root name on the front.

Subsequently, quilts from my maternal grandmother, Anna Green Godard, came into my possession. The family names include Green, Hayes, Allen, and Goodrich. Anna Godard; her mother, Emogene Hayes Green; her grandmother, Eliza Allen Green; and her great-aunt, Amelia Allen, were the makers of dozens of quilts in the Bushy Hill section of Granby where our ancestral home, which we still own today, is located. The men folk made their living by farming tobacco and trading horses. All of these quilts are beautifully backed with printed fabric—not a plain fabric among them! Included in this collection are quilt tops with little paper notes stitched on each, with salutations such as *To Ever from Aunt Amelia.* One may suppose that these were not quilted because several of these girls (my grandmother's sisters) never married, and, as was the custom of the times, tops were not quilted until the engagement was announced. Imagine our family's surprise when more quilts from this collection were found in 1991 in the attic of the ancestral home. They were all wrapped up with herbs and flower petals in an old trunk. Most of them were in unused condition and stored there for over one hundred years. In addition to the quilt collection, we found quilt pattern mock-ups in fabric and paper pieces, and, from her childhood, great-grandmother Emogene Hayes Green's sewing basket.

Additional quilts from my father's family, with the names Roffler, Fischer, and Sicknick, introduce a very different quality to this collection, as this branch of the family was from Germany and Denmark. These quilts were made in the United States with American patterns but with very different influences of color and fabric. The textiles used were not cottons but silks, satins, velvets, and wools. Colors were very bright pinks, yellows, and oranges. One quilt, a crazy quilt, is bordered with lace and also has matching pillow covers.

Bound by blood, birth, and soil, my ancestors inspired me to preserve this part of history for the family and community. The collection spans many generations and lives up to the calling that is shared by the family: to keep our heritage and pass it along.

Sawtooth Star, c. 1880, made by Amelia Allen (1837-1925), Granby, cotton, 81" x 83". Owned by great-great-grandniece, Carla Bue.

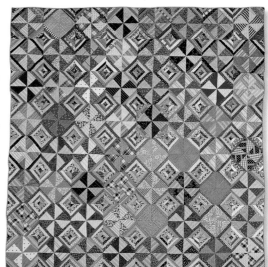

Pinwheel set in Squares, c. 1890, made by Lamira Viets Hayes (1835-1917), Granby, cotton, 77" x 78". Owned by great-great-granddaughter, Carla Bue.

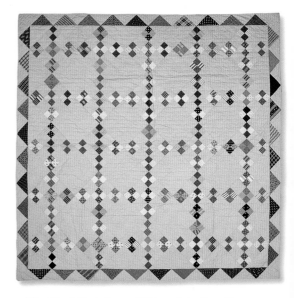

Nine-Patch Variation, c. 1920, made by Ever Green (1881-1955), Granby, cotton, 80" x 81". Owned by grandniece, Carla Bue.

Eliza Allen Green

Snowflake, c. 1850, made by Eliza Allen Green (1835-1923), Granby, cotton, 89" x 91". Owned by great-great-granddaughter, Carla Bue.

Emogene Cornelia Hayes Green

Log Cabin, Straight Furrow Variation, c. 1900, made by Emogene Cornelia Hayes Green (1856-1942), Granby, cotton, 75" x 77". Owned by great-grand-daughter, Carla Bue.

Ancestral home in the Bushy Hill section of Granby.

Polly Hall: Quilt Collector Extraordinaire

A familiar face in antique shops, church bazaars, and estate sales across Connecticut for the past twenty-five years is that of Polly Hall. Her quest was to acquire her own personal quilt collection. Known as the area's quilt lady, Polly was often approached by people whose family quilts were available to be purchased. Perhaps her love of quilts was first kindled with the Boston Pavement quilt made for Polly and her husband, Albert J. Hall, on the occasion of their wedding in 1940. The brightly colored cotton quilt has been kept in pristine condition and is one of Polly's most treasured possessions.

Polly was born in 1917. As an eighty-four year resident of Granby, she yearns to have time in her life to write about growing up in this little town near the Massachusetts border. As Polly stated, "I used to walk to school every day. Over the years, I knew where every wildflower grew along my path." Polly's sense of responsibility to societal issues began at the age of eight as a Girl Reserve in the Hartford County YWCA. During the 1940s, this organization arranged for inexpensive, safe living quarters for girls first moving into Hartford. She has continued her involvement over the past seventy-six years, serving finally as the Vice President of The Hartford County YWCA. Closer to home, she has been a dedicated member of Granby's Salmon Brook Historical Society and, on the political front, she is still active in the Republican Party. As Granby's Representative, she was elected to the State Legislature for two terms in the 1960s. Still intent upon serving in public office, she has been Justice of the Peace in Granby for many years, and her favorite duty is to perform marriages. Amazingly, Polly found time to raise her family of four children, all of whom received a college education. She was also a Charter Member of the Granby Tennis Club.

In 1976, Polly once again served her town, this time as Chairman of the Bicentennial Committee. It was then that her interest in quilting was piqued. After taking her first quilting lesson at The G. Fox & Company in Hartford, she made her first quilt. She joined her first quilt group at the South Congregational Church of Granby. They made flannel layettes to send to a New Delhi hospital. Polly fondly remembers that after many years and many India-bound care packages, the hospital nurses got up the courage to write and request that no more flannel layettes be sent. Apparently the very warm climate of India was not conducive to wearing flannel. After that, Polly began teaching her group to quilt as its new activity. Polly has made ten quilts herself and some have received blue ribbons.

Polly admits that her fascination with the variety of styles is what inspires her to collect quilts. Her collection began with an eighteenth-century copperplate and the number of quilts in her possession has now reached approximately one hundred. She longs to acquire a calamanco to complete the collection. Viewing her fabric medley, one appreciates Polly's eye for choosing stunning quilts.

Perhaps what really makes Polly Hall so special is her generosity in imparting her knowledge and love of quilts and quilting. Twice a year, when she "airs her quilts," she invites groups of quilters to view her collection. She takes the time to share the quilts' stories and what inspired her to make each quilt part of her collection. How lucky for the Connecticut quilt world to have Polly Hall in our midst with the limitless sharing of her love for quilting!

Boston Pavement, 1940, made by Victoria Howard, Ivoryton, cotton, 60.5" x 89". *Collection of Polly Hall.* Made for Polly's wedding.

Mosaic, c. 1876, maker unknown, Canton, cotton, 58" x 81". *Collection of Polly Hall.* The centennial fabric in this mosaic, English-paper pieced quilt top is what attracted Polly's eye. The light and dark arrangement of the mosaic honeycombs makes this top outstanding enough. Upon closer inspection, however, one finds fabric that was produced in 1876 in celebration of our nation's first birthday and the individual hexagons are just over one inch in size!

Pineapple, 1888, Canton, cotton, 88" x 93". *Collection of Polly Hall.* It was the historic narrative accompanying the Pineapple quilt that inspired Polly's purchase of this quilt. New Englanders are all too familiar with the Nor'easters, the winter blizzards that bury them in feet of snow. Housebound for three days during the blizzard of 1888, three Canton sisters made a quilt top each day. The deliberate placement of the blocks provides an illusion of the swirling of a snowy gale. In keeping with the construction of Log Cabin quilts, the top is pieced onto foundation fabric. The quilt was then simply bound with a commercial binding to make a lightweight quilt.

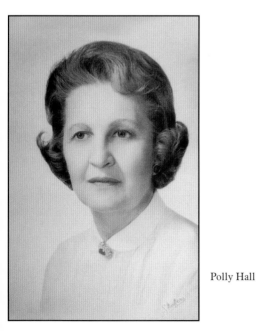

Polly Hall

161

What's Covering Connecticut*

by Susan Fiondella

D-day! October 2, 1992 and the small, quiet town of Washington, Connecticut, awaited the invasion of quilts and their owners for the first documentation day of The Connecticut Quilt Search Project (CQSP). It was the beginning of an accumulation of reams of data concerning pre-1950 Connecticut quilts and quiltmakers. From that first day through June 1, 1996, CQSP held twenty public and twenty-six private D-days. The information compiled from all the days fills fifty binders holding more than six thousand pages, with another eighteen binders securing over six thousand slides. The data from these pages forms the information base for this chapter, and the following sections briefly explore the data collected utilizing text and charts. The charts translate the data into percentages showing the specifics of the entire project by date range, the project totals as a whole, Connecticut totals, and other states' totals.[1]

"... and hanging overhead were gay bed quilts — the beautiful 'Wreath' with cradle quilt to match, the useful 'Diamond' quilt with a little one also, and the remarkable 'Stonewall' "
February 1, 1866

*This is an edited version of a more extensive body of work researched by the author.

Stone Wall, c. 1865-1890, Florence Briggs Haviland, Sherman, cotton, 80" x 90". Owned by Lenora Buck. In his book, *Connecticut Past and Present*, Odell Shepard wrote: "It was the stones of the place that whetted the wits of Connecticut inventors, turned us from agriculture toward the industrial life…" The dedicated farmers, however, cleared the land of the rocks and created a patchwork landscape with the stone walls they built. This quilt is a tribute to those stone walls.

Type

CQSP recorded 3,058 bed coverings, including quilts, quilt tops, tied comforters, summer spreads, and novelties. Of this group, 798 were documented or strongly attributed to Connecticut makers and 624 were made in "other states."[2] Unfortunately, over half of the items documented had no certain provenance. Therefore, in order to be statistically accurate, those quilts without a definite provenance were not considered either Connecticut quilts or quilts made in other states.

Signed/Dated

Signed quilts, with one or more signatures or initials, are important social records that supply the researcher with leads about the lives of women and their social/economic environment during a certain era. Of all the quilts documented in this project, 15% were signed and/or dated. The highest percentage occurred during 1840-1865 when 30% of the quilts were signed and/or dated. Similarly, just over half of Connecticut's quilts made between 1840-1865 were signed and/or dated while only 33% from other states had that distinction. Connecticut's high instance of making "signature" quilts from a variety of different patterns during this period secured the high rate of dated and/or signed quilts.[3] This inclination for signing and/or dating quilts continued into the next time period. Even though the overall percentage of signed and dated quilts decreased, the signing and/or dating of quilts that were not "signature" quilts *increased* from the previous period.

Format

As illustrated in Chart 2, most of the quilts documented were in the block format. By 1840-1865, block quilts—which displaced the whole-cloth quilt in the previous period—nearly doubled in popularity, becoming an American tradition. During each succeeding date range, the use of blocks remained above 70% except during 1925-1950; the decline during 1925-1950 was due to the use of the popular Double Wedding Ring pattern and the Grandmother's Flower Garden pattern, which are not block designs. Prior to 1865, the hexagon shape comprised most of the sample of mosaic all over designs. In the following decades, the introduction of new patterns like Tumbling Blocks and Tumbler, plus the continued use of an older

pattern known as Thousand Pyramids along with other one-patch designs, granted this format second place among quiltmakers. Prior to 1865, quilts with strip sets were found in Connecticut examples only. The medallion format had a steady use throughout the decades.

Block Design Sets

Blocks set edge-to-edge was the preferred design set among quiltmakers during all the decades except 1840-1865. During this period, the use of sashing prevailed—influenced by Connecticut quiltmakers' preference for that option. Sashing was first seen in Connecticut-made quilts between 1800-1840, but sashing on other states' examples did not appear until 1840-1865.

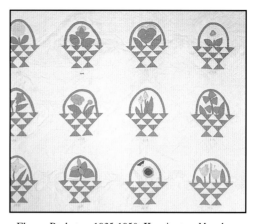

Flower Basket, c. 1925-1950, Kensington Monday Night Club, Kensington, cotton, 77" x 87". Owned by Berlin Historical Society. Formed in 1921 as a social sewing club, the Kensington Monday Night Club, still active today, has come to be known for its active role in charitable and community projects. This raffle quilt illustrates blocks placed on point with an alternate plain block set.

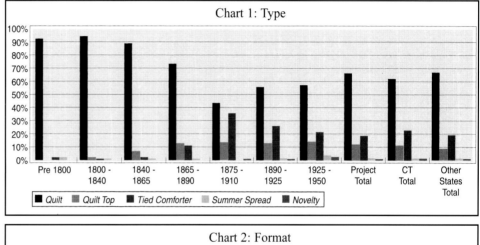

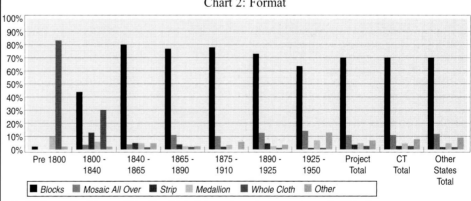

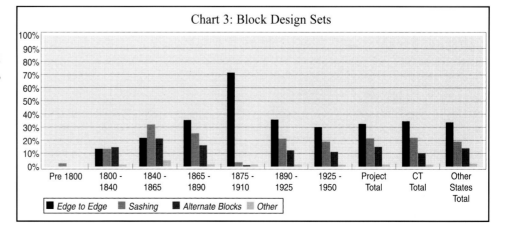

Union Square, c. 1840-1865, Sarah Harrison Beers, Cornwall, cotton, 87" x 88". Owned by Ann Gold. An illustration of garden maze sashing.

Construction Techniques

Quiltmakers created most of their designs by sewing fabric together by hand. The sewing machine aided in the production of 781 quilts. Completely machine sewn quilts numbered 342. In quilts displaying both methods, machine sewing was used primarily when making long seams such as borders and sashing. Appliqué quilts were trendy between 1840-1865 and 1925-1950, 11% and 10% respectively, while other periods recorded less than 5%.[4] In total, the percentages show that slightly more appliqué quilts and quilts with a combination of piecing and appliqué were made elsewhere. Blocks with embroidered motifs emerged between 1865-1890 and became fashionable from 1890 to 1950. Red embroidered motifs on white blocks, known as "Redwork," prevailed from 1890-1925. These quilts were more likely to come from Connecticut while other states had more quilts embellished with multi-colored embroidered motifs, popular from 1925-1950.[5]

Fabric Fiber, Prints, and Color

Cotton fabric dominated the majority of the bed coverings. Wool quilts prevailed prior to 1800, and quilts made entirely from linen numbered eight, with six dated prior to 1840. Silk, satin, and velvet fabrics comprised 10% of the collection and reflected a trend popular in the last quarter of the nineteenth century until circa 1910. Man-made fibers coexisted with natural fibers in 3.6% of the cases and were most evident from the turn of the twentieth century until 1950.[6]

Three-quarters of the quilts made in Connecticut and other states were scrap quilts using a variety of colorful prints and

Yankee Puzzle, c.1925-1950, Ellen Bertha Church Perkins, Groton, cotton, 50" x 76". Owned by Doris Griffin. Pieced by hand and treadle sewing machine, this top represents all quilt tops left unfinished that were completed by a future generation. Doris Griffin, Ellen's granddaughter, completed the top in 1992 by using a flannel sheet for the batting and a cotton backing. Ties hold the three layers together.

solids. The preference for combining solid and calico cloth continued throughout the nineteenth century to the end of the study period. In the middle of the nineteenth century, quiltmakers' second selection was to use only calico without any solid fabrics, and this option remained true until the second quarter of the twentieth century. Beginning in the 1920s and lasting to the end of the study period, quiltmakers returned to the pre-1950 trend of using only solid colored fabrics as their second preference.

Of the popular color combinations, the two-color blending tallied first and nearly 16% of the quilts possessed this distinction. The most prevalent two-color quilt was red and white, followed by blue and white, and then pink and white. Red and white was the first choice for two-color quilts between 1840 and 1925. In the last period, blue and white became the preferred color palette for two-color quilts. The red and white combination accounted for more than half of the two-color Connecticut quilts from 1840-1865 and no red and white quilts were found elsewhere. The three-color combination of red, green, and white peaked between 1840-1865. This combination was proportionally used more in other states' quilts than in Connecticut quilts. By the next period, this trio of colors lost favor. From 1925-1950, only Connecticut examples were in this color combination, while other states preferred pink, green, and white.

Sunflower, c.1800-1840, Eunice Hall, (1800-1867), Berlin, cotton, 87" x 87". Owned by Susan Fiondella. The Turkey red and yellow print maintains its vibrant colors and is most likely an imported fabric. The background lattice print is both roller printed and block printed. Sharp points and extremely fine stitching reveal that the maker was a skilled needlewoman.

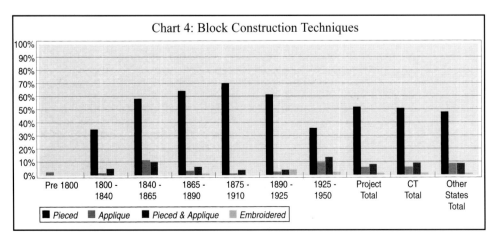

Chart 4: Block Construction Techniques

Pre 1800 | 1800-1840 | 1840-1865 | 1865-1890 | 1875-1910 | 1890-1925 | 1925-1950 | Project Total | CT Total | Other States Total

Pieced ▪ Appliqué ▪ Pieced & Appliqué ▪ Embroidered

Robbing Peter to Pay Paul, c.1840-1865, maker unknown, Goshen, cotton, 86" x 96" (reverse of the quilt shown in the backing section). Owned by The Goshen Historical Society. While most two color quilts use solid colored fabrics, this quiltmaker chose patterned goods.

Borders

Quilt borders trimmed 1,206 quilts (41%), and Connecticut quilts were almost as likely to have borders as were those from other states. The most favored border option was a single solid border on all four sides of the quilt.[7] Borders on three sides of the quilt prevailed from 1840-1865. Connecticut examples had a slightly higher usage of the single border treatment, while multiple border treatments showed a slightly higher percentage on other states' quilts.

Orange Peel, c. 1865-1890, made by Gracia Sperry Bunce, Milford, cotton, 86" x 86". Owned by Robert J. Sperry. An illustration of a quilt with borders on three sides. Legend has it that this classic quilt pattern was created when the Marquis de Lafayette was paying a triumphal visit to the United States in 1824-1825. In Philadelphia, he was the honored guest at a banquet where oranges imported from Barcelona were served. The Marquis peeled an orange skin away in four equally divided sections. One of the ladies attending the banquet asked to receive this pared skin as a souvenir, which she took home and from the oval pieces made a quilt pattern.

Backing and Batting

The most common backing or lining fabric used was cotton, with synthetics, silk, linen, and wool also represented. Of the lined bed coverings, slightly more than half consisted of a solid colored fabric, but prints and weaves were also discovered. Printed linings became increasingly common between 1865-1925, accounting for nearly 50% of the backs during these years and numbering almost two to one over the preceding or succeeding years.

Cotton was the most widely used filler. Wool filled 106 quilts spanning all the time periods, but was most prevalent prior to 1800. Blankets appeared fifty-six times and flannel sheeting twelve times; they were used primarily between 1925-1950. Nearly four hundred items contained no filler.

Backing on Robbing Peter to Pay Paul, c. 1840-1865, maker unknown, Goshen, cotton, 86" x 96". Owned by The Goshen Historical Society. Descended through the family of Alice M. Spaulding Johnson (1848-1929). The design has a late eighteenth-century English feel, but the piece, while not lacking in design quality, has a crude block cutting and poor mixture of color, giving it an American attribution with a date of 1800-1850.

Quilting

Hand quilting surpassed machine quilting forty to one. Most work was simple, using a combination of lines including grids, chevron, clamshell, circle, and chains, and the surface coverage was light to average. Many times the lines were used in conjunction with simple floral, geometric, or pictorial motifs. Elaborate quilting appeared in only 5.5% of the quilts. Heavy quilting using simple designs covered 16% of the pieces. Connecticut quilts were not likely to be heavily quilted or quilted with fancy patterns—this distinction was left to other states' quilts. Connecticut quiltmakers preferred simple lines or lines with other motifs with a modest to moderate density. Five hundred fifty bed coverings were tied with pearl cotton, wool, or silk threads.

Pineapple, c. 1890-1925, maker unknown. Owned by The Bristol Historical Society. An illustration of machine quilting.

Patterns

Project quilts made in the block format numbered 2,068. A total of 529 different patterns were used, but more than three-quarters of the block quilts were made using one of only 193 patterns. In each date range, quiltmakers continued to use patterns from earlier time periods as well as newly

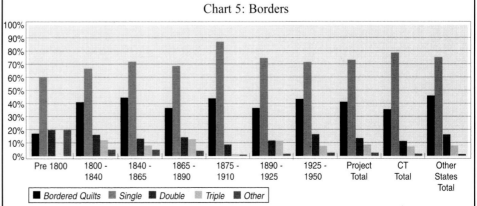

Chart 5: Borders

Legend: Bordered Quilts, Single, Double, Triple, Other

X-axis: Pre 1800, 1800-1840, 1840-1865, 1865-1890, 1875-1910, 1890-1925, 1925-1950, Project Total, CT Total, Other States Total

developed patterns. The quilting revival of the early twentieth century is distinctly apparent in the 209 new block patterns that appeared between 1925-1950.

The Album pattern emerged during 1840-1865. Just over 20% of Connecticut quilts made in 1840-1865 used this pattern while other states realized only 7.5%. The Log Cabin pattern appeared from 1865-1890. It continued through the next period and represented nearly 10% of the quilts made during these decades. Crazy quilts, those made of silk, satin, and velvets embellished with fancy embroidery stitches, became a fashion trend from 1875-1910. More Crazy quilts came from other states than from Connecticut.

While the Dresden Plate pattern was the most popular block pattern in the 1925-1950 date range, it ranked third among the chosen patterns for that period. Quiltmakers departed from using the block style during this time and returned to a mosaic One-Patch pattern. Grandmother's Flower Garden was the most preferred pattern, followed by the Double Wedding Ring pattern, another non-block pattern. The only pattern used multiple times by Connecticut quiltmakers but not seen in other states' quilts was "Yankee Puzzle." How appropriate![8]

Conclusion

The purpose of this chapter was to report the statistical findings of the Connecticut Quilt Search Project, to (1) verify style, patterns, color, and quilt development in specific date ranges, and (2) analyze information that would unveil a typical or trendy quilt that was positively Connecticut.

The second objective proved more difficult to attain. Statistically, nothing specific stood out as a truly Connecticut innovation in quiltmaking. The development of quiltmaking was influenced by many factors. Each state or region of the United States had its own political, social, and industrial growth that affected the women who lived there and the kinds of quilts they made. The top choices in each category reveal that quiltmakers were making similar quilts in each respective period. Women who quilted usually made what was popular, while frequently employing their own variations to express their personal taste.

Early Connecticut quilts were exemplified by the wholecloth style and block designs set straight either edge-to-edge, with sashing or an alternate plain block. Between 1840-1865, sashing between blocks adorned just over half of Connecticut-made quilts and appears to be a Connecticut fashion statement. During this period and after, regionalism in quilt patterns and styles became homogenized due to the advancements in transportation and communication. Subsequently, a traveler spending the night at a Connecticut inn snuggled under a Connecticut quilt would not see many differences between this quilt and one made in his or her own state.

Once the block format was introduced, the variations in design sets simultaneously appeared and quiltmakers used them to express individual taste. As early as 1806, Connecticut quiltmaker Catherine Selleck made a block quilt. It was a simple Nine-Patch set with alternate plain blocks (see page 17). From this humble beginning, the block designs exploded into intricate patterns. The reason for the leap from making wholecloth quilts to block quilts is not known. So far, no early-published source of block patterns has been found. Early quilts, however, had elements of the block style, which may have been the catalyst for this invention. While community living in Connecticut, characterized by shared work, was a social reason that fueled and sustained this method of quiltmaking, it is still unclear how it started.

The scope of the data makes it difficult to draw conclusions without more specialized research. Perhaps closer inspection will divulge how Connecticut's evolution influenced its quiltmakers, or if Connecticut, along with other New England states, functioned as part of a larger region having more in common with each other than by themselves. Hopefully, further investigation will complement existing research, add to the knowledge of quilts, and generate new areas of study.

Chart 6 — Summary Data

	Pre 1800	1800-1840	1840-1865	1865-1890	1875-1910	1890-1925	1925-1950	Project Total	CT Total	Other States Total
Origin										
Connecticut Totals	11	33	107	142	55	152	276	776		
Other States Totals	1	6	39	72	61	117	307	603		
Unknown Totals	17	85	224	348	178	313	419	1584		
Project Totals[9]	29	124	370	562	294	582	1002	2963		
Type										
Quilt	27	118	330	415	142	330	584	1946	480	411
Quilt Top	0	4	26	72	42	81	145	370	82	57
Tied Comforter	1	1	11	68	106	154	209	550	180	114
Summer Spread	1	1	3	7	1	12	36	61	18	14
Novelty	0	0	0	0	3	5	28	36	16	7
Total	29	124	370	562	294	582	1002	2963	776	603
Signed/Dated										
Dated Only	1	2	5	8	28	8	14	66	20	15
Signed Only	3	8	40	30	40	31	26	178	62	25
Signed and Dated Only	1	7	65	36	46	26	30	211	90	43
Total Signed and/or Dated	5	17	110	74	114	65	70	455	172	83
Border Techniques/ Single Border										
Solid	3	19	39	78	85	115	221	560	131	136
Pieced	0	10	34	43	22	30	37	176	53	35
Appliqué	0	5	44	22	2	11	38	122	28	31
Other	0	0	3	3	6	3	13	28	10	5
Edge Finishes										
Applied bias	0	3	18	49	18	48	203	339	70	102
Applied straight	2	64	230	285	39	191	259	1070	295	189
Back folded to front	2	3	29	62	32	121	154	403	104	108
Edges butted	15	14	11	29	52	74	109	304	100	52
Front folded to back	4	8	10	25	17	20	34	118	26	29
Woven tape	0	17	25	4	2	6	6	60	17	8
Piping	0	0	5	0	0	2	1	8	3	1
Fringe	2	3	0	3	1	0	1	10	2	1
Prairie points	0	0	0	0	1	3	7	11	2	5
Lace	0	0	0	1	21	1	2	25	10	1
Other	1	0	8	12	29	13	18	81	17	12

The Memories

D-Days! Planning, anticipation, excitement, exhaustion! All were rewarding, all gave us a sense of doing something worthwhile, and through the quilts we experienced the creativity, love, dedication, and resourcefulness of the quiltmakers. We also experienced very valuable life lessons. What follows are reflections by some of the Project members themselves.

CQSP banner at the first Documentation Day, October 3, 1992, Washington, Connecticut.

"There is a definite side effect to quilting: friendship. When I became involved with CQSP, along with three other quilting enthusiasts from my area, I had no idea that for the next five years I would be cementing quilting friendships into a support group. At least once a month we traveled the state together. With four women in one car, on round trips of up to four hours, there was always one of us with a child crisis, family illness, or joyous occasion to share. We laughed and cried, gave and received advice, helped to deal with grief and encouraged each other when decisions needed to be made. This was a mobile therapy group. And during the documentation day itself we were participating in the lives of the women who made the quilts. Whether they were intricate, well designed quilts or patched and thrown together quilts, each had its own story, which we had the privilege of being a part of."
—Betsey Henebry

"Each D-Day brought me in contact with colleagues eager to learn, with owners eager to share, and with quilts that always had something to teach me if I looked closely enough. At all of our D-Days we had a ribbon set up to minimize traffic in the analysis area and, as I was looking at a signature on the back of a quilt, a woman was leaning over the ribbon. I asked if the quilt was hers and when she said it was, I invited her to take a closer look. She was thrilled to find out it was signed and was going home to find out more about the quiltmaker. It was a joy for our team to be part of her discovery."
—Tora Sterragaard

"Participating in CQSP for nearly ten years was a rewarding venture that provided personal growth and invaluable experiences. Every D-Day brought a different challenge and something new

to learn about quilts, textile identification, and history.

When researching in libraries and historical societies in order to piece together the stories for the book, every discovery about a quilt, quiltmaker, or related event in state or town history was a joy that cannot be explained. As a life long resident of Bristol, Connecticut, I now have a new appreciation for my hometown and state and the people who shaped them.

When I first joined the Project, everyone involved was a stranger to me. Now, after years of working together on a shared interest, I have been blessed with long lasting friendships for which I am truly thankful."
—Susan Fiondella

"Upon attending my first CQSP meeting in 1992, I was very impressed with the dedication and commitment the members showed to assure the success of this project. My husband Stan volunteered to drive me to the many D-Days and once there, he too became caught up in the project and remained to become one of the volunteers. I will most remember discovering how rich our state is in antique quilts and how we might have lost this heritage had it not been for the dedication of members who persevered and brought the project to a successful conclusion."
—Wanda Stolarun Dabrowski

" 'Say QUILT' calls out the photographer. The documentation team is grouped for the formal photo at the beginning of the day's activities. In this one moment, those being photographed are closely drawn together and recorded as part of our history. Viewed through the camera lens, we are a kaleidoscope of colors, patterns, hairdos, and faces, all of which form our own unique quilt-for-a-day pattern. We are unique as single pattern pieces and we are pieces of the whole. It showed in our work during the day. As a quilt gives warmth, we gave confidence and support to each other in every phase of the documentation process."
—Marie MacDermid

"My feelings regarding D-Days have been one of 'touching history.' I learned so much from quilters of long ago. Their quilts 'spoke to me' and I felt so very proud to be a very small link in the chain of women who have made quilting history. Seeing, touching, and admiring their work was an outstanding experience!"
—Pat Glaser

"My fondest and most vivid recollections are those of the D-Days I was privileged to attend. Though no two locations were the same, each was set up to permit the easy passage of quilts through the process leading to examination of the quilts. It was gratifying to be a part of this important exercise, to associate with women who shared so willingly and pleasantly their knowledge of quilts with those of us who were less well informed."
—Elizabeth Bellach

"I will never forget my first documentation day in the picturesque town of Woodstock, Con-

necticut. The date was November 7, 1992 at the First Congregational Church. I had the opportunity to do the oral history and meet so many enthusiastic and friendly ladies. They were all eager to share stories about their personal quilts. The women of the church graciously welcomed CQSP with a delicious luncheon and all were right there to take care of our every need. It was a full and busy day in a most lovely setting."
—Cynthia Warren Mahdalik

"For me the quilt search has been very exciting: the contacts with other quilters, the beautiful and interesting quilts, and even the not-so-beautiful ones. Overriding all is the admiration and appreciation for all of the people who have guided and pushed this project along. It is mind boggling to consider the hours spent in preparation for D-days. I have great appreciation for the whole group and its efforts."
—Lucy Davis

"I have never gone somewhere and not learned something new, and the tiny village of Northfield was no exception to the rule. That particular D-Day was held in an eighteenth-century church where I was assigned to hold quilts up for photography. Two small details had skipped my attention. First, at 5'2" most of the quilts were at least 3 feet longer than I was! Secondly, the photo area was two flights of narrow eighteenth-century stairs above the rest of the process! Nearly 200 quilts held high above my head later, I had learned some important things about life, as well as quilting: Laugh more and stretch a little—reach beyond your limit. Admire how you're put together more than how you look, as strength outlives beauty. Be humbled by history and be proud to be a part of it. Don't overlook anyone—all people and all things have a story to share. Listen to the whisper of the subtle and the small, adrift amid the shouting of a larger world. You'll be surprised at what you'll learn."
—Peg Pudlinski

"Over the span of the project many changes took place in our personal lives and within our families. Our children grew, went off to college, married, grandchildren came, beloved members of our families and wonderful friends left us, we changed careers and even retired. Time passed rapidly as we faced the ups and downs of our lives. As we planned and implemented the different phases of the project, many times I wondered if we would reach our goal. The gratification of working together as a team throughout the span of years was reinforced by the sharing of our individual stories, the support we gave to each other, the beautiful quilts we saw, and the joyous response of the quilt owners who shared a piece of their personal family history with us. Many were amazed to think that a group of total strangers could be so interested in a quilt or a life that they only knew as a name or a faint remembrance from childhood. Joy, pride, and appreciation of the precious gift left to them were expressed by smiles, hugs and tears. Indeed, changes did take place in our lives! Thank you everyone for making this experience a special gift to me."

—Elizabeth Tishion

"When we moved to Connecticut in 1980, it was like moving backwards in time. For eleven years prior to that our family lived in Northeastern Ohio, also known as Connecticut's Western Reserve. This is where my interest in quilting began during my years as a young mother. However, it wasn't until our family came to Connecticut that quilting touched my woman-soul.

A very dear friend, Polly Jewett, and I held a quilt show in the Church on the Green in Washington, Connecticut and from that success a group called The Meetinghouse Quilters developed. Their generosity, kindness, and support have shined continually on the Connecticut Quilt Search Project over the past years. Through raffle quilts, sponsorship of the first D-Day, co-hosting a Holiday Tea and reception, volunteering at the Gala, these women just gave and gave. I will always be grateful for their support.

Taking part in over forty D-Days, both public and private, afforded us an opportunity to crisscross our beautiful state. The memories of these wonderful days and the women and men who assisted us will not fade for many, many years."

—Sue Reich

"When The Connecticut Quilt Search Project first began over ten years ago, little did any of us know of the exciting journey that lay ahead. Any project of this size could not exist without its share of trials and tribulations, and we certainly have had ours, but overall it has been my experience that it was a positive, rewarding, and spiritually satisfying endeavor. To touch and feel and speculate about something that was made 50, 100, 150 years ago, and to think about the person who created it, made me feel very proud and somewhat awed to have taken part in this project. It is my firm belief that all the women (and men) who toiled and strived to create these wonderful quilts are surely resting more comfortably knowing that their work will always be a part of history. Whether the quilt was a humble utilitarian one just made to provide warmth, or whether it was made as an outstanding example of the quilter's skills, they were all made with love! Love of family, love of beauty, and love of quilting!

It has been my good fortune to be associated with a wonderful group of devoted, selfless people who have spent countless hours to insure the success of this project. This truly was a team effort and absolutely everyone involved has made a contribution to its success."

—Maureen Gregoire

Crazy Quilt, c. 1875-1890, made by Mary Eliza Potter Spencer (1853-1909), velvet and silks, 65" x 69". Owned by Martha L. Kneen. Mary Eliza Potter was born in Moodus in 1853. She married James Frederick Spencer around 1870 and together they raised three children in the town were James's ancestors were among the first settlers in 1662. The sunflowers, daisies, strawberry blossoms, pansies, floral sprays, butterflies, and fancy stitches dance around the quilt and make you believe that Mary wanted to capture the beauty of a garden in full bloom. Framed with a pieced border of lozenge shapes and fans to cool one in the summer's heat, she continued to embellish the outlines giving it that special touch.

Harriet Walker Dart

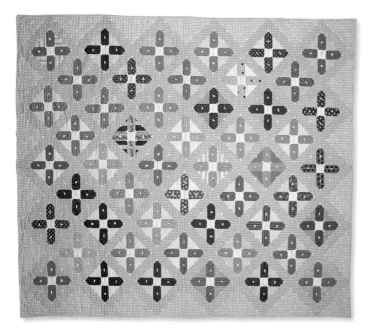

Snowflake Signature, c. 1886, made by The Ladies' Aid Society of Vernon Congregational Church, Vernon, cotton 90" x 106". Owned by Frank H. and Claire Niederwerfer. Harriet Walker Dart was born on December 3, 1836. She married George Trumbull Skinner on August 15, 1859 and they had one daughter, Hattie Louise, in 1863. George was struck by lightning about ten years later and was institutionalized. Harriet is considered the maker of this large quilt, but in reality she had plenty of help. The quilt was made by the Ladies' Aid Society of the Vernon Congregational Church as a fundraiser. This quilt was raffled off and won by Albert C. Dart, a son-in-law of Harriet's, and descended in the family to its current owner: a great-great-grandson of Harriet's. A Dart family member entered the quilt in the Tolland County Farm Bureau Field Day and Exhibit in 1937, where it took First Prize.

168

Documentation Days, Sites, Sponsoring Organizations, and Coordinators

October 3, 1992
First Congregational Church, Washington, Meetinghouse Quilters: Janet Strausberg and Sue Reich

November 7, 1992
First Congregational Church, Woodstock, Woodstock Hill Quilters: Lucy Davis

February 6, 1993
South United Methodist Church, Manchester, Mulberry Quilters: Marge Knight and Maureen Gregoire

March 6, 1993
Canoe Brook Senior Center, Branford, The Shoreline Quilters: Marilyn Barba

April 17, 1993
Noah Webster House, West Hartford, Quilters' West and the West Hartford Quilters: Sally Williams

May 22, 1993
North Street School, Greenwich, The Historical Society of the Town of Greenwich: Barbara Freeman

June 12, 1993
Noank Firehouse, Noank, Noank Historical Society: Holly Simons

September 18, 1993
Northfield Congregational Church, Northfield, Northfield Historical Society: Jan Nicholson and Lillian Olmstead

October 2, 1993
St. Mary's Church Hall, Jewett City, Country Quilters of Northeast Connecticut: Cindy Rizer and Sue Tiffany

November 6, 1993
First Congregational Church, Vernon, Ellington Country Quilters and Vernon Country Quilters: Carolyn Bunick

February 5, 1994
Kensington United Methodist Church, Kensington, Sisters in Quilting, SQ Chapter of the Greater Hartford Quilt Guild: Joyce Ryeeck

March 19, 1994
South Congregational Church, Hartford, South Congregational Church: Barbara Field and Janet Wallace

April 16, 1994
Newtown Congregational Church, Newtown, The Nutmeg Quilters: Heloise Wilkinson

May 14, 1994
Portland Senior Center, Portland, The Heart of the Valley Quilters: Janet Ross and Mary Hurlberg

June 4, 1994
Hoxie Firehouse, Mystic, North Stonington

Historical Society: Rita Elliot

September 17, 1994
St. Theresa's Parish Center, Granby, The Granbees: Lucille Ladden

November 12, 1994
The Covenant Congregational Church, Easton, The Trumbull Piecemakers: Marilyn Cocking

February 11, 1995
The First Congregational Church, Cheshire, The Village Green Quilters: Cynthia Sawyer

May 20, 1995
First Baptist Church, Essex, The Shoreline Quilters: Sue Robinson and Deidre Stow

June 1, 1996
Mohawk Ski Lodge, Cornwall, Woodridge Quilters of Goshen and The Northwest Corner Quilters Guild: Barbara Hammerstrom, Jill Gibbons, and Corinne Levy

Museums, Historical Societies, and Private Documentation Days

October 24, 1992, Bristol Historical Society, Bristol
November 11, 1994, J and N Fabric Shop, Clinton
April 25, 1995, Connecticut Historical Society, Hartford
May 5, 1995, Bristol Chapter, Greater Hartford Quilt Guild, Bristol
August 1, 1995, Gunn Museum, Washington
October 7, 1995, Stratford Historical Society, Stratford
October 24, 1995, Simsbury Historical Society/ Polly Hall Collection, Massacoh Plantation, Simsbury
February 10, 1996, Lyman Allen, New London
February 27, 1996, Goshen Historical Society, Goshen
March 3, 1996, Bates-Scofield House, Darien Historical Society, Darien Goodwives
March 9, 1996, Danbury Museum and Historical Society, Danbury
March 9, 1996, Museum of the New Haven Colony, New Haven
March 12, 1996, Keeler Tavern, Ridgefield
March 12, 1996, The Historical Society of the Town of Greenwich, Greenwich
May 8, 1996, The New Milford Historical Society, New Milford
May 13, 1996, Sherman Historical Society/The Buck Family Collection, Sherman
July 24, 1996, Wethersfield Historical Society, Wethersfield
July 30, 1996, Thomaston Historical Society, Thomaston
August 5, 1996, Mansfield Historical Society, Mansfield
August 13, 1996, African-American Quilts, New Haven
August 15, 1996, Henry Whitfield State Historical Society, Guilford
August 15, 1996, Hyland House, Guilford
August 15, 1996, Thankful Arnold House, East

Haddam
September 10, 1996, Torrington Historical Society, Torrington
September 12, 1996, Sharon Historical Society, Sharon
September 30, 1996, Norfolk Historical Society, Norfolk

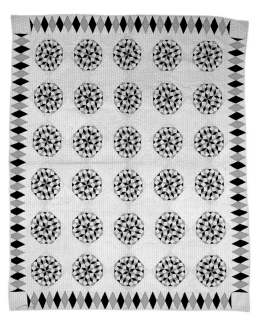

Carpenter's Wheel Variation, c. 1865-1890, made by Pearl N. Munday (1885-1951), cotton, 72" x 83.5". Owned by Norma Munday. The pencil markings for the elaborate quilting are still visible.

Oak Leaf Appliqué, maker unknown, c. 1860, cotton, 82" x 83". Given to the Sherman Historical Society by the Cannon family of Sherman. This quilt bears a striking resemblance in style and fabric to a blue and white Oak Leaf quilt in the collection of the Metropolitan Museum of Art. The museum's quilt was featured in *American Quilts and Coverlets* and made in Duchess County, New York; the western border of Sherman.

A Legacy

The Connecticut Quilt Search Project was founded with the following goals:

· To document and preserve the histories of Connecticut quilts and quiltmakers.
· To encourage the art of quiltmaking.
· To educate the public in the conservation and care of quilts.
· To promote good fellowship among all who love and appreciate quilts.

We hope that with the publication of this book our goals have been met, however, the story of Connecticut's quilts and quiltmakers does not end here.

All of the material collected over the past ten years will be archived at the Connecticut Historical Society in Hartford, Connecticut. To facilitate the work of future quilt researchers and historians, a program will be endowed in conjunction with the Connecticut Historical Society (and funded by the proceeds of this book) to enable present day quiltmakers and collectors the opportunity to register their quilts, old and new. This Quilt Registry Legacy is our gift to the quiltmakers and quilt owners of our state for ten years of generous support and cooperation in the making of this book.

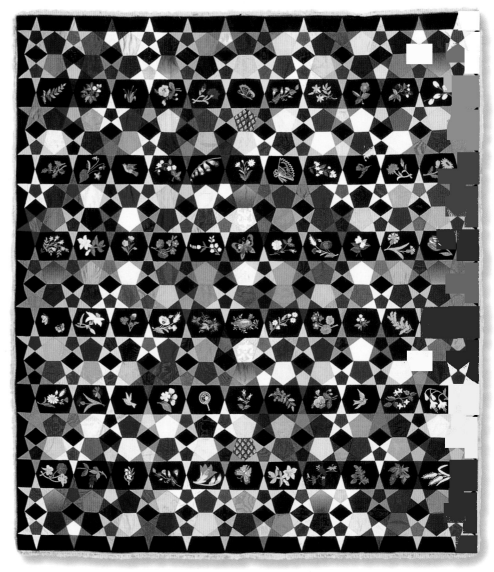

Star of the West, 1875, made by Susie C. Walker, Manchester, satin and silk, 55" x 62". Owned by The Cheney Homestead of the Manchester Historical Society.

Endnotes

Note: The sources for some of the material in the quiltmakers' biographies are from family memoirs, family records, and genealogical studies.

Historic Sampler
[1] Ellen D. Larned, *History of Windham County, Connecticut* (Ellen D. Larned, 1880), p.395.
[2] Ibid.
[3] Ibid., p. 395.
[4] *Litchfield County Centenniel Celebration* (Hartford Edward Hunt, 1851), p. 112.
[5] John Warner Barber, *Connecticut Historical Collections, History and Antiquities of Every Town in Connecticut with Geographical Descriptions*, p. 92.
[6] Rev. Alonzo B. Chapin, *Glastenbury for Two Hundred Years: A Centennial Discourse* (Press of Case, Tiffany and Company, 1853), p. 125.
[7] Mary Caroline Crawford, *Social Life in Old New England* (1914), p. 432-33.
[8] Kate Brannon Knight, *History of the Works of Connecticut Women at the World's Columbia Exposition: Chicago, 1893* (Hartford, Conn., 1899), p. 37.

Mary Geer Denison
[1] Richard Anson Wheeler, *History of the Town of Stonington, First Settlement in 1649 to 1900* (Lawrence Verry Incorporated, 1966), p. 137.
[2] Ibid., p. 138.
[3] James Geer, *Historical Sketch and Genealogy of George & Thomas Geer from 1621 to 1856* (Elihu Geer Printer, Hartford), 1856.
[4] Walter Geer, *The Geer Genealogy* (New York, Bretanos, 1923), p. 28-29.
[5] Ibid., p. 29.

Beulah Galpin Merriam
Source: Connecticut Revolutionary War Records, Beardsley memorial Library, Winsted, Connecticut.

Ruth Benton Thompson
[1] Rev. A.G. Hibbard, *History of the Town of Goshen, Connecticut* (Press of Case, Lockwood & Brainard Company, 1897), p. 535.
[2] *Litchfield County, Centennial Celebration, 13th and 14th of August, 1851* (Hartford Edwin Hunt, 1851), p. 123.
[3] Hibbard, *History of the Town of Goshen, Connecticut*, p. 300.
[4] Information from family records.

Asenath Rising
[1] Cameron Haight King, *The King Family of Suffield, Connecticut* (San Francisco, CA. 1908), p. 110.
[2] *Celebration of the Two Hundred and Fiftieth Anniversary of the Settlement of Suffield, Connecticut, October 12, 13, and 14, 1920* (Authority of the General Executive Committee, 1921), p. 81.
[3] Joseph Anderson, *The Town and City of Waterbury, from the Aboriginal Period to the Year Eighteen Hundred and Ninety-Five* (The Price & Lee Company, 1896), p. 524.

Catherine (Caty) Selleck
[1] Selleck family Memorial Book.
[2] Elizabeth Gemming, *Wool Gathering* (Coward, McCann & Geoghegan, 1979), p. 12.

Betsey Smith Paine
[1] Lyman May Paine, *My Ancestors, A Memorial of John Paine and Mary Ann May of East Woodstock, Conn.*, Private Circulation, 1914, p. 33.
[2] John C. Pease and John M. Niles, *A Gazetteer of the States of Connecticut and Rhode-Island*

(William S. Marsh, 1819), p. 226.
[3] Ellen Larned, *History of Windham County, Connecticut* (Published by the Author, 1880), p. 451.
[4] Pease and Niles, *A Gazetteer of the States of Connecticut and Rhode-Island*, p. 226.

Ann Ingersoll Brush
Source: *Supplement l & ll. to The Descendants of Thomas and Richard Brush of Huntington, Long Island*, Compiled by Stuart C. Brush , (Gateway Press, 1995, 1001 N. Calvert St., MD 21202).

The Jerusha Clark Peck Wedding Quilt
[1] Theodore and Nancy Sizer, Sally Schwager, Lynne Templeton Brickley, Glee Krueger, *To Ornament Their Minds: Sarah Pierce's Litchfield Academy 1792-1833* (The Litchfield Historical Society, 1993), p. 114-136.
[2] Harriet Beecher Stowe, *The Minister's Wooing* (A.L. Burt Company Publishers, 52-58 Duane Street, New York 1875), p. 246-247.
[3] *The Hartford Times; List of early Connecticut Marriages*, Connecticut State Library.
[4] William H. Russell, *Peck, A Sketch* (Los Angeles, CA, 1922).
[5] *Church Membership, Congregational Church Records*, Connecticut State Library.
[6] Edward Atwater, The *History of the City of New Haven to the Present Time* (W.W. Munsell, New York 1887), p. 441.

Sarah "Sally" Plant Judson
[1] Rev. Samuel Orcutt, *A History of the Old Town of Stratford and the City of Bridgeport, Connecticut* (Fairfield County Historical Society, 1886), p. 1098.
[2] Linda-Jeanne Dolby, *Descendants of William Judson of Connecticut*, Connecticut State Library, p. 96.
[3] Wilcoxson, *History of Stratford, Connecticut, 1639-1939*, p. 745.
[4] Orcutt, *A History of the Old Town of Stratford and the City of Bridgeport, Connecticut*, p. 1099.

From Dress Cloth to Bed Cloth
[1] Stephen S. Marks, *Fairchild's Dictionary of Textiles* (Fairchild Publications, Inc., 1959), p. 96.

Louisa Brigham
[1] Bruce Fraser, *The Land of Steady Habits, A Brief History of Connecticut* (Connecticut Historical Commission and Hartford, Connecticut 1988), p. 157.
[2] Abram Foote, *Foote Family Comprising the Genealogy and History of Nathaniel Foote, Vol.I* (Gateway Press, Inc. Baltimore, 1984), p. 17.

Sarah Fish Lord and Lydia Lord
[1] John C. Pease and John M. Niles, *A Gazetteer of the States of Connecticut and Rhode Island* (William A. Marsh, 1819), p. 154.

Sarah Edmond Booth
[1] The League of Women Voters of Newtown, *Newtown, Connecticut Past and Present*, 1934.
[2] James Hardin George, Allison Parish Smith, Ezra Levan Johnson, *Newtown's Bicentennial* (The Tuttle, Morehouse, & Taylor Company, 1906), p. 85.
[3] Jane Eliza Johnson, *Newtown's History and Historian Ezra Levan Johnson* (The Historian's Life Companion, 1917), p. 200.

Mabel Ruggles Canfield
Source: Litchfield Historical Society Archives.

The Charter Oak
[1] Katharine Stanley Nicholson, *Historic American Trees* (Frye Publishing Company, 1922), p. 12.
[2] John Warner Barber, *Connecticut Historical Collections, History and Antiquities of Every Town in Connecticut* (Durrie & Peck and J.W. Barber, 1836), p. 43-44.
[3] Supplement to the *Courant*, August 20, 1856.
[4] Nicholson, *Historic American Trees*, p. 14.
[5] Ibid.

The Hollister Family Chintz Quilt
[1] D. Hamilton, *History of Litchfield County, Connecticut* (J.W. Lewis & Co. 1881), p. 174.
[2] Ruth Barnes Moynihan, *Coming of Age; Four Centuries of Connecticut Women and Their Choices* (Connecticut Historical Society, 1991), p. 35.
[3] Lieut. John Hollister, compiled by Lafayette Wallace Case, M.D., *The Hollister Family of America* (Fergus Printing Company, 1886), p. 382 and 394.

Clarinda Beers McKay
[1] Danbury Head Stone Inscriptions, Danbury Museum and Historical Society.

Content Newton
[1] Caroline Gaylord Newton, *Rev. Roger Newton and one line of his Descendants* (1912), p. 54.
[2] Ibid., p. 55.
[3] Joseph Anderson, *The Town and City of Waterbury, Connecticut, from the Aboriginal Period to the Year Eighteen Hundred and Ninety-Five, Vol. III* (The Price & Lee Company, 1896), p. 539.
[4] Caroline Gaylord Newton, *Rev. Roger Newton and one line of his Descendants*, p. 163.

Henrietta Frances Edwards Whitney
[1] Jonathan Edwards Woodbridge, *The Memorial Volume of the Edwards Family Meeting at Stockbridge, Mass.* (Congregational Publishing Society, 1871), p. 173.
[2] John W. Barber, *History and Antiquities of New Haven, Conn.* (L.S. Punderson and J.W. Barber, 1856), p. 47.
[3] John W. Barber, *Connecticut Historical Collections, History and Antiquities of Every Town in Connecticut* (Durrie & Peck and J. W. Barber), p. 184.

The First Independent Universalist Church
[1] Donald Watt, *From Hersey Toward Truth*, The Universalist Church of West Hartford, Connecticut, 1971, p. 79.
[2] Watt, *From Hersey Toward Truth*, p. 80.

Eliza Jane Bishop Judson
[1] Connecticut Historical Commission, *Historic Resources Inventory Buildings and Structures*, 1991-92, No. 275.
[2] *Woodbury Land and Deed Records*, Connecticut State Library.
[3] William Cothern, *History of Ancient Woodbury, Connecticut, from The First Indian Deed in 1659 to 1854, including the Present Towns Washington, Southbury, Bethlem, Roxbury, and a part of Oxford and Middlebury* (Reprint, Genealogical Publishing Co. Inc., 1977), p. 238.
[4] *Memoirs of the Eliza Jane Bishop Judson family*.

Esther Scofield Sands
[1] Darien Museum and Historical Society Archives

Mary Katherine Sands Bibbins
[1] Darien Museum and Historical Society Archives

The Mead Quilts from Fairfield County
[1]Daniel M. Mead, *The History of Greenwich, Fairfield County, CT. With Important Statistics* (New York: Baker & Goodwin, Printers, 1857), p. 15.
[2]Spencer Percival Mead, *History and Genealogy of the Mead of Fairfield County, Connecticut, Eastern New York, Western Vermont, and Western Pennsylvania from A.D. 1180 to 1900* (The Knickerbocker Press, 1901), p. 124-125.

The Zachariah Ferris Quilt
[1]Russell B. Noble and Minot S. Giddings, *Two Centuries of New Milford, Conn, The Story of New Milford told in Chronological Epitome* (The Grafton Press, 1907), p. 98.
[2]Remembrance from family history provided by Donald Marsh, February 2000.
[3]Ibid.
[4]Samuel Orcutt, *History of the Town of New Milford and Bridgewater, Connecticut 1703-1832* (Press of the Case, Lockwood and Brainard Company, Hartford, 1882), p. 596.

Cynthia Wells Standish
[1]The Leaves of the Tree, A Pageant in Celebration of the Tercentenary of Wethersfield, Connecticut given on June 8 and 9, 1934, Connecticut Historical Society.
[2]Genealogies and Biographies of Ancient Wethersfield, Wethersfield Historical Society.
[3]Gladys Macdonough, *The Stone and The Spirit, A Walking Tour Guide to the Ancient Burying Ground in the Wethersfield Village Cemetery* (Wethersfield Historical Society, 1987).

Sarah Lewis
[1]Rapt in a Quilt of Greenwich History, Susan Richardson (*Greenwich Magazine*, November 1992), p. 109-117.
[2]*One Hundred and Fiftieth Anniversary of the Second Congregational Church of Greenwich, Conn.* (New York: Clark & Maynard Publishers, 1867), p. 66.
[3]Ibid., p. 75.
[4]*One Hundred and Fiftieth Anniversary of the Second Congregational Church of Greenwich, Conn.*, p. 76.

Sarah Jane Barnes' Trousseau Quilts
[1]Helen Hunt W. Humphrey, *Sketches of Roxbury, Conn.* (The Times Print Shop, New Milford, CT, 1924), p. 15-17.
[2]Jan Cunningham and Elizabeth Warner, *Historical and Architectural Survey of the Town of Roxbury, Connecticut* (Cunningham Associates, LTD., Middletown, Connecticut, 1996-7).
[3]Barbara Jean Mathews, *The Diary of Col. Albert Hodge (1756-1842)* (Gateway Press, Inc. Baltimore, MD. 1992), p. 126-127.

Sarah Mary Stevens Bailey
[1]The Commemorative Biographical Record of Middlesex County, Connecticut (Chicago J.H. Beers & Co., 1903), p. 793-94.
[2]*Tin History*; Commemorative Biographical Record of Middlesex County, p. 793.

Robert Lauder Mathison
[1]Guide to New Milford, Connecticut and its environs; Including Washington, Roxbury, Bridgewater, Kent, Sherman, Warren, p. 78.
[2]Arthur Godenough, *The Clergy of Litchfield County* (Litchfield County University Club, 1919), p. 131.

Mary Esther Hoyt Smith
[1]Norwalk Historical and Memorial Library, *Norwalk After Two Hundred and Fifty Years* (C.A. Freeman, 1901), p. 381.

Sisters! Let us gird ourselves anew!
[1]*The Ladies Benevolent Association of Northfield, CT, February 1, 1866*, Litchfield Historical Society.
[2]*The One Hundredth and Fiftieth Anniversary of the Second Congregational Church of Greenwich* (New York: Clark & Maynard Publishers, 1867), p. 78.
[3]Connecticut Quilt Search Project, *Puzzler Quilts and Other CQSP Oddities*, 1999.

Medallion Baby Quilt
[1]Harriet Beecher Stowe, *The Minister's Wooing* (James R. Osgood and Company, Boston, 1875), p. 435.
[2]Grace Rogers Cooper, *The Copp Family Textiles* (Smithsonian Institute Press, Washington, D.C., 1971), p. 5.

Post Civil War Sampler
[1]*Nov. 3, 1863, Records from the Secretary's Book of the Ladies Benevolent Society of Northfield, 1842-1865, Vol. I*, Litchfield Historical Society, Litchfield, Connecticut.
[2]*April 14, 1863, Records from the Secretary's Book of the Ladies Benevolent Society of Northfield, 1842-1865, Vol. I*, Litchfield Historical Society, Litchfield, Connecticut.
[3]*Nov. 3rd, 1863, Records from the Secretary's Book of the Ladies Benevolent Society of Northfield, 1842-1865, Vol. I*, Litchfield Historical Society, Litchfield, Connecticut.
[4]*The Sanitary Commission Bulletin, New York, January 15, 1864*, Connecticut State Library, p. 164.
[5]*May 10th,1865, Constitution on The Ladies Benevolent Association, at Northfield, CT. 1865-1886, Vol. II*, Litchfield Historical Society, Litchfield, Connecticut.
[6]*September 13th, 1866, Constitution on The Ladies Benevolent Association, at Northfield, CT. 1865-1886, Vol. II*, Litchfield Historical Society, Litchfield, Connecticut.
[7]*July 7th, 1867, Constitution on The Ladies Benevolent Association, at Northfield, CT. 1865-1886, Vol. II*, Litchfield Historical Society, Litchfield, Connecticut.
[8]*Nov. 1881, Constitution on The Ladies Benevolent Association, at Northfield, CT. 1865-1886, Vol. II*, Litchfield Historical Society, Litchfield, Connecticut.
[9]*Jan. 1883, Constitution on The Ladies Benevolent Association, at Northfield, CT. 1865-1886, Vol. II*, Litchfield Historical Society, Litchfield, Connecticut.
[10]*1885, Mar. 19th, Constitution on The Ladies Benevolent Association, at Northfield, CT. 1865-1886, Vol. II*, Litchfield Historical Society, Litchfield, Connecticut.
[11]*Foreign Missionary Society, Account Book 1815-1834*, Second Congregational Church of Greenwich, Connecticut (Historical Society of the Town of Greenwich).
[12]John Warner Barber, *Historical Collections, History and Antiquities of Every Town in Connecticut* (Durrie & Peck and J.W. Barber, 1836), p. 422.
[13]Marvis Olive Welch, *Prudence Crandall, a Biography*, p. 11.
[14]Clarence Winthrop Bowen, *The History of History of Woodstock, Connecticut* (The Plimpton Press, 1926), p. 627.
[15]Jack Larkin, *The Reshaping of Everyday Life 1790-1840*, p. 299.

Lois Hotchkiss
[1]Sarah J. Prichard and others, Edited by Joseph Anderson D.D., *History of Waterbury, Vol. 1* (The Price & Lee Company, 1896), p. 520.
[2]Ibid., p. 417.
[3]Ibid., p. 520.
[4]Ibid., p. 524.

[5]Ibid., p. 523.
[6]Ibid., p. 525.
[7]Ibid., p. 544.
[8]Katherine A. Prichard, *Ancient Burying-Grounds of the Town of Waterbury, Connecticut* (The Mattatuck Historical Society, 1917), p. 64.

Humphreysville Album Quilt
[1]Ellsworth Grant, *Yankee Dreamers & Doers* (The Connecticut Historical Society & Fenwick Productions, 2nd Edition), p. 45.
[2]Francis Little, *Early American Textiles* (The Century Company, New York/London, 1931), p. 110.
[3]Albert E. Van Dusen, *Connecticut,* (Random House, NY, 1961), p. 186.
[4]Lewis Sprague Mills, *The Story of Connecticut,* (Richard R. Smith, West Rindge, New Hampshire, 1958), p. 342.
[5]Steve Dunwell, *The Run of The Mill,* (David R. Godine, Boston, Massachusetts, 1978), p. 19.
[6]Mills, *The Story of Connecticut,* p. 360.
[7]Ibid., p. 360.
[8]Grant, *Yankee Dreamers & Doers,* p. 45.
[9]Caroline F. Ware, *New England Cotton Manufacture,* (Russell & Russell, New York, 1931), p. 142. Reference from: *American Wool & Cotton Report, Vol. XIV, 1900, p. 170.*
[10]Grant, *Yankee Dreamers & Doers,* p. 45.

Mary A. Beers
[1]Newspaper article accompanying the quilt at the Stratford Historical Society

Henrietta Smith Glover
[1]D. Hamilton Hurd, *History of Fairfield County, Connecticut* (J.W. Lewis, 1881), p. 424.
[2]Ibid.

Mary Ann Hoadley Seymour Tomlinson
[1]Frances Atwater, *History of the Town of Plymouth* (Higginson Book Company, 1895), p. 236-37.
[2]Frances Bacon Trowbridge, *The Hoadley Genealogy, A History of the Descendants of William Hoadley* (Printed for the Author, 1894), p. 69.

Nellie L. Gates Ransbotham
[1]I would like to thank Mr. Paul Crunden, a long time resident of Hartland, for the pleasant walk over the area to verify the location of the mill site.

Sarah Elizabeth Allyn Latham
[1]James D. McCabe, *The Illustrated History of the Centennial Exhibition* (The National Publishing Company, 1876), p. 333.

Gertrude Fyler Hotchkiss
Source: Torrington Historical Society Archives.

The Universalist Social Benevolent Society and The Ladies Benevolent Association of the Second Ecclesiastical Society of Suffield
[1]Donald Watt, *From Heresy Toward Truth*, The Universalist Church of West Hartford, 1971, p. 115.
[2]Ibid., p. 116.
[3]Ibid., p. 107.
[4]Ibid., p. 116.
[5]Records from the West Suffield Congregational Church.
[6]Ibid.
[7]Ibid.
[8]Ibid.

"We are all Crazy"
[1]Stephen Collins, *Danbury Crowned Them All;*

Hatting in Danbury, Danbury Scott-Fanton Museum, 1966. Truman Warner, *Danbury, Three Hundred Years of Change and Growth*, (Danbury Publishing Division, Ottaway Newspapers, Inc. 1983), p. 29.

[2]James Montgomery Bailey/Susan Benedict Hill, *History of Danbury, Conn. 1684-1896* (Burr Printing House, 1896), p. 453.

[3]Ibid., p. 448.

[4]*Newstimes*, April 7, 1885, p.3.

[5]Bailey/Hill, *History of Danbury, Conn. 1684-1896*, p. 451.

[6]Ibid., p. 452.

[7]*Newstimes*, April 2, 1885, p. 3.

[8]*Newstimes*, April 14, 1885, p. 3.

[9]*Newstimes*, April 16, 1885, p. 3.

[10]*Newstimes*, April 16, 1885, p. 3.

[11]Bailey/Hill, *History of Danbury, Conn. 1684-1896*, p. 452.

[12]Ibid., p. 254.

Lucretia Norton Carlisle Tuttle

[1]Diary of Lucretia Norton, Goshen Historical Society, Goshen, Connecticut.

[2]Rev. A.G. Hibbard, *History of the Town of Goshen, Connecticut*, (Press of The Case, Lockwood & Brainard Company, 1897), p.107.

Emma Tracy Baldwin Gold

[1]Wm. T. Cogsweel, Esq., *History of Rockville from 1823-1872*, 1872.

[2]Michael R. Gannett, *The Cream Hill Agricultural School, West Cornwall, CT*, Cornwall Historical Society, 1986.

[3]W. F. Whipple, Connecticut State Grange, *The Connecticut Granges*, 1900, p. 28.

Ann Elizabeth Morehouse Prindle

[1]*Lakeville Journal*, March 27, 1952, Jean Fulcher.

[2]Joel Benton, *Amenia Seminary Reunion, August 22d, 1906* (Broadway Publishing Company, New York 1907), p. 21.

[3]*Lakeville Journal*, March 27, 1952, Jean Fulcher.

[4]*Lakeville Journal*, August 14, 1947, p. 29.

[5]*Lakeville Journal*, March 27, 1952, Jean Fulcher.

Nella Babcock Branford

[1]John Warner Barber, *Connecticut Historical Collections, History and Antiquities of Every Town in Connecticut* (Durrie & Peck, and John Warner Barber, 1836), p. 434.

[2]The Assembly Book and Connecticut Public Register 1895.

Laura Electa Seymour

[1]George Dudley Seymour, *The Seymour Family* (New Haven, Connecticut, 1939), p. 527.

[2]*Souvenir of the Centennial Exhibition of Connecticut's Representation at Philadelphia, 1876*, (Geo. D. Curtis, Hartford, Connecticut), 1877, p. 124 and 233.

[3]Seymour, *The Seymour Family*, p. 527.

Susan Hill Buck

[1]New Milford Historical Society Records, *Obituary, Susan Hill Buck*, December 1904.

[2]Notes from the Centennial Exhibit regarding a pair of trousers won by Dr. George Taylor at age 2.

[3]Arranged and Compiled by Samuel Buck of Crown Point, N.Y., *Origin and Genealogy of the Buck Family*, 1917, p. 51.

[4]Ibid., p. 51.

[5]Howard Peck, *Howard Peck's New Milford, Memories of a Connecticut Town* (Phoenix Publishing 1991), p. 43.

[6]New Milford Historical Society Records, *Obituary, Susan Hill Buck*, December 1904.

Mrs. K. H. Colvin

Source: *Commemorative Biographical Record of Tolland and Windham Counties/Connecticut* (J.H. Beers & Co., Chicago), 1903, p. 1021, 1246, 1247.

The Bunnell Family

[1]*Needlecraft Magazine*, Nov.1931 p. 16.

The Morgan Sisters

[1]Kiracofe, Roderick, *The American Quilt, A History of Cloth and Comfort 1750-1950* (New York Clarkson Potter, 1993), p. 146.

Woman's Relief Corps

[1]Bristol Centennial Celebration 6/17/1885, compiled by John J. Jennings (Press of the Case, Lockwood and Brainard Co., Hartford, Conn., 1885), p. 90.

Myra Lord Converse

Source: Commemorative Biographical Record of Tolland and Windham Counties/Connecticut (J.H. Beers & Co., Chicago, 1903).

[1]Earl M. Witt, *Town of Stafford, 250th Anniversary Committee, 1969*, (Town of Stafford).

Angie Estelle Goodwin

[1]The Dresden Plate pattern made up of spokes or petals arranged in a circle included eight to twenty spokes. Assortments of fabric scraps were available for purchase through magazine ads and quilt pattern books; ready-cut or die cut pieces in the desired shape were also available. Other pattern names evolved by altering fabric placement or color scheme: Friendship Ring, Aster, Grandmother's Sunbonnet, and Grandmother's Sunburst.

Cornelia Ball Jenks

Source: Torrington Vital Records and Torrington Company Records.

Stella Jewett Godard

[1]Jewett Genealogy provided by the Salmon Brook Historical Society, p. 844.

[2]Deborah Harding, *Red & White, American Redwork Quilts* (Rizzoli International Publications, Inc., 2000), p. 21.

[3]Information provided by the Salmon Brook Historical Society.

[4]Information provided by the Salmon Brook Historical Society.

Under the Red Cross Flag

[1]American Red Cross, Virtual Museum, 1900-Present.

[2]Patrick Gilbo, *The American Red Cross, The First Century* (Harper & Row, Publishers, 1981), p. 5-32.

[3]History of Hartford Chapter American National Red Cross, June 1919, Connecticut State Library, Hartford, Connecticut.

[4]Helen Frost and Pam Knight Stevenson, *Grand Endeavors, Vintage Arizona Quilts and Their Makers* (Northland Publishing, 1992), p. 78.

Lucy Leete Bishop

[1]John Warner Barber, *Connecticut Historical Collections, History and Antiquities of Every Town in Connecticut* (Durrie & Peck and J. W. Barber, 1836), p. 216.

[2]Mary Hoadley Griswold, *Yester-Years of Guilford* (The Shore Line Times Publishing Company, 1939), p. 38.

[3]Ibid., p. 81.

Minnie Pearl Pardee Barrett

[1]Barbara Brackman, *Old Patchwork Quilts and the Woman Who Wrote It, Quilter's Newsletter Magazine*, Nov-Dec/88, p. 37.

Gladys Hall Melius

[1]*Needle Craft Magazine*, May 1931, p. 31.

Maie Mallette

Source: Torrington Vital Records.

Frances Lucy Guinchi Baldi

[1]Quilt kits were packaged and sold by mail order companies and department stores. They included fabric and instructions needed to complete the quilt. Not all kits produced a wholecloth design like this one. Kits also consisted of block designs for piecing and appliqué.

Sarah Eva Watrous Pomeroy

[1]Remembrances of Catherine Pomeroy Fields, Sarah's daughter.

Gathered Pieces

[1]Wanda Stolarun Dabrowski, *Research of Connecticut Quilts in Collections Outside Connecticut*, 1998. This is an edited version of a more extensive body of work researched by the author.

What's Covering Connecticut

[1]The project totals include the totals for known Connecticut quilts, known other states' quilts, and all the quilts with unknown provenance that were recorded in specific date ranges.

[2]CQSP documented almost as many known quilts from other states and Canada as known Connecticut quilts. Many have been in Connecticut a long time, but provenance reveals that they were made elsewhere. In the text, the phrase "other states" is used to indicate all the quilts documented in the project that were made elsewhere.

[3]Notably throughout the Project, Connecticut "signature" quilts utilized 31 different block patterns while other states used only 6 different patterns.

[4]The fashion for red, green, and white appliqué quilts between 1840-1865 was the determining factor for the increase in this period, since 62% of the appliqué quilts were in this color combination. Between 1925-1950, Sun Bonnet Sue and Butterfly patterns accounted for 26.5% and floral appliqué designs made up 44% of the appliqué patterns.

[5]Nine of the 31 Redwork quilts were dated: the earliest date was 1883, the latest date was 1918. Of the 26 embroidered quilts from 1925-1950, five were dated: the earliest date was 1932, the latest date was 1946.

[6]A visual analysis of the fibers was relied on since time constraints did not allow viewing the fibers under a microscope.

[7]A "solid" border refers to one piece or strip of fabric regardless of its print or color.

[8]Nearly one-quarter of the quilts in the block format are pieced in one of these patterns: Album, Log Cabin, Crazy, and Dresden Plate.

[9]Project totals include only the quilts that were documented in the designated date ranges. There were 95 quilts documented that had to be excluded from the study because they did not meet the date range criteria.

Bibliography

Album of Jane M. Seymour, 1822-1827, The Litchfield Female Academy.

Album of Jane Maria Seymour, Litchfield, CT. 1824-1825, Litchfield Historical Society.

Album of Mary Bassett, The Litchfield Female Academy.

Andrews, Kenneth R. *Nook Farm, Mark Twain's Hartford Circle*. University of Washington Press, 1950.

Atkins, Jacqueline Marx. *Shared Threads, Quilting Together Past and Present*. Viking Studio Books, 1994.

Barber, Elizabeth Wayland. *Woman's Work, The First 20,000 Years*. Norton, 1994.

Beecher, Catharine and Harriet Beecher Stowe. *The American Woman's Home*. J. B. Ford & Co., 1869.

The Bi-Centennial Committee. *Bicentennial Celebration, July 6th, 7th, 1908*. The Case, Lockwood & Brainard Co., Hartford, CT, 1908.

Bingham, Harold. *History of Connecticut*. Lewis Publishing, 1962.

Bliss, Rev. Daniel. *Church Life, 1954 Annual Report*. The Second Congregational Church of Greenwich, CT.

Brackman, Barbara. *Encyclopedia of Pieced Patterns*. American Quilter's Society, Paducah, KY, 1993.

Buel, Joy Day and Richard Buel, Jr. *The Way of Duty; A Woman and Her Family in Revolutionary America*. W.W. Norton and Co., 1984.

Burpee, Charles W. *The Story of Connecticut. Volumes 1-4*. The American Historical Company, Inc., 1939.

Bushman, Richard. *From Puritan to Yankee; Character and Social Order in Connecticut 1690-1756*. W.W. Norton, 1970.

Caroline Boardman's Journal, Litchfield June 1, 1815, Litchfield Historical Society.

Clarissa Collins Journal, 1825, Connecticut Historical Society.

Clark, Ricky, George W. Knepper & Ellice Ronsheim. *Nineteenth & Twentieth Century Quilts, Quiltmakers and Traditions*. Rutledge Hill Press, 1991.

Comp, A. *History of Litchfield County, Connecticut*. J.W. Lewis and Company, 1881.

Connecticut Historical Society. *Prospectus of Mr. Emerson's Female Seminary at Wethersfield, Connecticut, 1826*, Connecticut Historical Society.

Corcoran, Rachel, Rita Erickson, Natalie Hart, Barbara Schaffer. *New Jersey Quilts 1777 to 1950, The Heritage Quilt Project of New Jersey*. American Quilter's Society, 1992.

Delaney, Edmund. *Life in the Connecticut Valley 1800-1840, From the Recollections of John Howard*. Connecticut River Museum. Essex, CT. 1988.

Delia Seymour's Album, 1835-1832, The Litchfield Female Academy. Litchfield Historical Society.

Diary of Charlotte Maria Smith (while attending school in Litchfield) Litchfield Historical Society, 1824-1825.

Elisha Sheldon, Hand Written Note, Elizabeth Sheldon Peck, Litchfield Historical Society.

Evans, Sarah M. *Born For Liberty; A History of Women in America*. The Free Press, 1989.

Fennelly, Catherine. *Connecticut Women in the Revolutionary Era*. Pequoit Press, 1975.

Ferrero, Pat, Elaine Hedges, Julie Silber. *Hearts and Hands, The Influence of Women & Quilts on American Society*. The Quilt Digest, 1987.

Finley, Ruth. *Old Patchwork Quilts and the Women Who Made Them*. J.B. Lippincott, 1929.

Forrest, John and Deborah Blincoe. *The Natural History of the Traditional Quilt*. The University of Texas Press, 1995.

Fox, Sandi. *For Purpose and Pleasure, Quilting Together in Nineteenth Century America*. Rutledge Hill Press, 1995.

Grant, Ellsworth S. *The Miracle of Connecticut*. The Connecticut Historical Society, 1992.

Harper's New Monthly Magazine, Volume LVL, December 1877 to May 1878, Harper & Brothers, Publishers, New York, 1878.

Hofstadter, Richard, William Miller, Daniel Aaron. *The United States: The History of the Republic*. Englewood Cliffs, NJ: Prentice Hall, Inc., 1967.

Horton, Laurel. *Quiltmaking in America: Beyond the Myths*. Nashville, TN: Rutledge Hill, 1994.

Jennie S. Wetmore. *Diary, Lebanon, Conn., July 1857*. Connecticut Historical Society

Johnson, Alexander. *Connecticut, A Study of a Commonwealth Democracy*. Houghton Mifflin and Company, 1887.

Kilborn, Payne Kenyon. *Town of Litchfield, Connecticut*. Press of Case, Lockwood and Brainard Company, Hartford, 1882.

Kolter, Jane Bentley. *Forget Me Not, A Gallery of Friendship and Album Quilts*. The Main Street Press, 1985.

Langdon, William Chauncy. *Everyday Things in American Life, 1776-1876*. Charles Scribner and Sons, 1941.

Letter from Emily Hart to Mrs. Ruth Norton, Berlin, CT. Litchfield, Aug. 10th, 1830. Litchfield Historical Society.

Lindsey, David. *Ohio's Western Reserve*. The Press of the Western Reserve, 1955.

Lipman, Jean and Alice Winchester. *The Flowering of American Folk Art 1776-1876*. The Whitney Museum of American Folk Art, Courage Books, 1974.

Litchfield Historical Society. *A Guide to Local Historical and Genealogical Resources in Northwest, CT*. Litchfield Historical Society, 1993.

Loring, James. *The Girl's Best Ornament with other Sketches*. Sabbath School Book-Store, Boston, 1832.

Macgill, Patrick. The Great Push; An Episode of War. http://raven.cc.ukans.edu/~kansite/ww_one/memoir/macgill.html.

Matthews, Glenna. *Just a Housewife, The Rise and Fall of Domesticity in America*. Oxford Press, 1987.

Matthews, Glenna. *The Rise of Public Woman, Woman's Power*. Oxford University Press, 1992.

McKim, Ruby Short. *Designs Worth Doing, Fall and Winter Catalogue 1931-32*. Artcraft Department, Everyday Life, Chicago, IL.

Monat, Emilie. *Connecticut State History of the Daughters of the American Revolution*. Finlay Brothers, 1923.

Montgomery, Florence. *Printed Textiles, English and American Cotton and Linens 1700-1850*. Viking Press, NY, 1970.

Morse, Jarvis Means. *A Neglected Period of Connecticut's History, 1818-1850*. Yale University Press, 1933.

Moynihan, Ruth Barnes, Cynthia Russett, Laura Crumpacker. *Second to None; A Documentary History of American Women Volume 1: From the 16th Century to 1865*. University Press of Nebraska, 1993.

Newcomb, Sarah Ann Weaver. *Recollections of a Long Life, 1914*. Autobiography.

Osborn, Norris Galpin. *History of Connecticut in Monographic Form*. The States History Companion, 1925.

Peck, Amelia. *American Quilts and Coverlets, The Metropolitan Museum of Art*. New York: Dutton Studio Books, 1990.

Perry, Charles E. *Founders and Leaders of Connecticut*. D.C. Heath and Company, 1943.

Phelps, Charles Shepard. *Rural Life in Litchfield County*. The Litchfield County University Club, Norfolk, CT., 1917.

Sanford, Elias B. *History of Connecticut*. S.S. Scranton and Company, 1887.

Sarah Beekman's Journal, 1807, May-August, Litchfield, Litchfield Historical Society.

Satve, Bruce. *Mills and Meadows, A Pictorial History of Northeastern Connecticut*. The Donning Company, 1991.

Severa, Joan. *Dressed for the Photographer*. The Kent State University Press, 1996.

Shepard, Odell. *Connecticut Past and Present*. Alfred A. Knopf, 1933.

Skylar, Kathryn Kish. *Catharine Beecher, A Study in American Domesticity*. W.W. Norton & Company, 1976.

Spaulding, J.S. *Illustrated Popular Biography of Connecticut*. Case, Lockwood and Brainard Co., 1891.

Stephenson, George M. *The Puritan Heritage*. The MacMillan Company, 1952.

Strand, Sharon. *Many a Drunkard Slept Under a Drunkard's Path Quilt, The Use of Material Culture as Non-Verbal Rhetoric by the Woman's Christian Temperance Society*. Black Hills State University, 1999.

The History of the Town of Litchfield, Connecticut, 1720-1920, Enquirer Print 1920.

The Union Signal, September 8, 1877, Collection of Sue Reich.

Theriot, Nancy. *Mothers and Daughters in Nineteenth Century America*. University Press of Kentucky, 1996.

Vanderpool, Emily Noyes. *Address by John P. Brace, Teacher, October 28, 1816, More Chronicles of a Pioneer School from 1792-1833*. Cambridge, MA: The University Press, 1927.

Walters, Ronald G. *American Reformers 1815-1860*. Hill and Wang, 1978.

Warren, Elizabeth V. and Sharon L. Eisenstat. *Glorious American Quilts, The Quilt Collection of the Museum of American Folk Art*. Penguin Press, 1996.

White, Alain C. *The History of the Town of Litchfield, Connecticut, 1720-1920*. Enquirer Print 1920.

Woodard, Thos. K. & Blanche Greenstein. *Twentieth Century Quilts*. E.P. Dutton, 1988.

World Book Encyclopedia. Chicago, IL: World Book, Inc., 1995.

Zeichner, Oscar. *Connecticut's Years of Controversy 1750-1776*. Institute of Early American History and Culture at Williamsburg, Virginia, University of North Carolina Press, 1949.

Index of Quiltmakers and Quilt Patterns

Epitaph

Ruth Snow Bowen

As the postmistress of Chaplin, one room of Ruth Bowen's house was the town's Post Office where she received and distributed the mail of eastern Connecticut. When people came to have their letters posted, they could also watch the progress of Ruth's latest quilt laid out in her dining room. Ruth always had a quilt in the making—in her ninety-year lifetime, she finished over 300 quilts and all were Grandmother's Flower Gardens!

A life-long church member of the Chaplin Congregational Church, Ruth was active in the Women's Fellowship and was the organist for her church. For her musical contribution, Ruth refused to accept any money, saying that her work was for Jesus. A 1950 article about quilting in *Life* magazine reported on Ruth and her quilting spirit. By 1979, her quilt count was 261, as recollected by Mrs. Theresa Ridgeway of Chaplin.

Ruth died on October 10, 1983, but her love for quilting is immortalized on her grave stone in the Old Cemetery in Windham. On her tombstone is engraved "The Quilt Lady," an appropriate title for one of Connecticut's most prolific quilters.

Grandmother's Flower Garden, c. post-1950, made by Ruth Snow Bowen (1895-1983), Chaplin, cotton, 86" x 99". Owned by Julie Ristow LaCava. Although this quilt is post-1950, it is the only one of Ruth's three hundred quilts that the Project was able to locate.